# THE LIFE AND HISTORY OF
# NORTH AMERICA'S
# INDIAN
# RESERVATIONS

# THE LIFE AND HISTORY OF
# NORTH AMERICA'S INDIAN RESERVATIONS

## GENERAL EDITOR: RICHARD PARCHEMIN

JG PRESS

This edition was first published in 1998 by
PRC Publishing Ltd., Kiln House,
210 New Kings Road, London SW6 4NZ

Published in the USA 1998 by JG Press
Distributed by World Publications, Inc

The JG Press is a trademark of JG Press, Inc
455 Somerset Avenue, North Dighton, MA 02764

This edition was produced by American Graphic Systems, Inc. San Francisco USA

Design © 1998 American Graphic Systems, Inc.

Designed and captioned by Bill Yenne, with design assistance from Azia Yenne
and proofreading by Andy Roe and Joan B. Hayes.
Special thanks to Andy Roe and Bill Yenne for writing and/or editing substantial portions of the text.

ISBN 1–57215–255–9

Printed and bound in China

*Page one:* A delegation of representatives of Plains tribe reservations in
Washington in June 1880. Included are Nakananitien of the Kiowa-
Apache, Wild Horse of the Comanche, Stumbling Bear of the Kiowa
and Taodaiko of the Wichita. Standing in the background are Bureau of
Indian Affairs Agent F.B. Hunt and E.L. Clark, an interpreter.

*Page two:* A Native American dancer in rapt concentration at the annual Red Earth Festival in Oklahoma City.

NOTES ON TERMINOLOGY:
The term "Indian" has been in use for centuries to describe the people
who are more descriptively called "Native Americans." While the latter
term has gained favor recently in academic circles, the older term is still
in use by tribal organizations, United States and Canadian government
institutions, and the people themselves. For the purposes of this book,
they are used interchangeably.
    The term "Indian reservation," or, in Canada, "Indian reserve,"
defines a specific area of land which has been "reserved," set aside or
acquired for the occupancy and use of an Indian tribe or a group of
tribes. In some cases, groups smaller than tribes are referred to as bands,
and areas smaller than reservations may be referred to as communities,
colonies or villages. In California, the Spanish term "rancheria" is used.
    Tribal names have also undergone recent changes. The term "Eskimo"
has been entirely replaced by "Inuit," which is the peoples' name for
themselves. The Sioux people once referred to themselves as "Dakota"
(or, depending on region, "Lakota" or "Nakota"). However, the term
"Sioux" is still in use officially. We have used one or the other as seemed
appropriate in context. The Navajo call themselves "Dinneh," meaning
"the people," but "Navajo" is still the official term and we have used it
throughout.
    In some cases, different but similar terms are used to describe the
same people. Examples are "Kootenai," "Kutenai" or "Kootenay;" "Mohican," "Mohegan" or "Mahican;" "Miwok" or "Me-Wok;" and "Ojibwa" or
"Ojibway."
    In some cases, we have adopted certain conventions in spelling, such
as choosing "Navajo" over "Navaho;" or "Mohave" over "Mojave."

ACKNOWLEDGEMENTS:
The editors wish to thank the United States Bureau of Indian Affairs and
Canada's Department of Indian and Northern Affairs for supplying
research materials which made this book possible. Thanks also to all the
government and other agencies and companies listed below, who gener-
ously supplied the photographs used in this book.

PICTURE CREDITS:
All of the photographs were supplied by the National Archives, with the
following exceptions:

Alaska Division of Tourism: 117, 118, 119 (both), 120, 123, 124 (both),
        125 (top)
American Graphic Systems Archives: 20-21, 26, 27, 30, 31, 36, 37, 42-
        43, 46-47, 66-67, 106, 107
Arizona Office of Tourism: 98 (top), 99 (bottom)
Grand Casino Avoyelles: 127, 128, 129
Grand Casino Mille Lacs: 130, 133
Florida Division of Tourism: 156, 157, 161
© Tom Gerczynski, via Fort McDowell Casino: 131, 132
Library of Congress: 18, 19, 61, 89, 94, 96, 102, 114-115 (all)
Louisiana Office of Tourism: 145 (top)
Maryland Office of Tourism: 138
Fred Marvel, Oklahoma Tourism: 2, 140, 153
Montana Department of Commerce: 142, 149, 150 (top), 151 (top)
National Anthropological Archives: 1, 8, 17, 33, 44, 45, 53, 60, 65, 85,
        86, 86-87, 101 (bottom), 104 (bottom), 105 (top), 113, 122,
        178, 183, 192
North Carolina Travel and Tourism: 146, 160, 162
Oklahoma Tourism: 14
US Department of the Interior: 15, 64, 68, 69, 70, 71 (both), 72, 73, 97
        (both), 108-109, 136-137, 138-139, 141, 142-143, 146-147
Virginia Division of Tourism: 135, 154, 155
Western Museum of Ethnography: 10, 11, 20, 33,34, 39, 66, 78, 79, 112
© Bill Yenne: 74-75 (all), 101 (top), 103, 104 (top), 104-105, 108, 111,
        148-149, 150-151, 158-159 (all), 163

# TABLE OF CONTENTS

# INTRODUCTION

Before attempting to discuss North America's native people, or to define their identity, it is important to clarify basic terminology. Are they Indians or Native Americans? When the indigenous people of North America were first encountered by Europeans, the latter thought that they had arrived in the East Indies, and therefore believed that the people were "Indians." Even after it was determined that a new continent had been discovered, the term Indian remained in use. In the 1980s, the more descriptive term "Native American" also entered the lexicon, although tribal organizations, United States and Canadian government institutions and the people themselves tended to favor the older term. Today, both are in use, and for the purposes of this book, they are used interchangeably.

In terms of a definition, an Indian reservation, or in Canada, an Indian reserve, is a specific area of land which has been "reserved," set aside or acquired for the occupancy and use of an Indian tribe or a group of tribes. Throughout North American history, reserves and reservations have been created for several purposes. Initially, they were created to reduce the land area used by Native Americans. Later many reservations were set up as sites for the relocation of Indian tribes being moved westward to make room for the white settlers.

In some cases, reservations were designated as places for the confinement of Native Americans who resisted the westward expansion of the non-Indians. Many reservations were set aside as places of sanctuary to protect Indians from non-Indians or from more aggressive

tribes. Most of the twentieth century reservations have been acquired or set aside as a base for economic development.

To examine the history of Indian reservations (in Canada, reserves), from their early beginnings in the mid-nineteenth century to the present, is to explore a complex and often tragic episode of North America's past. What we discover is the inevitable clash of two cultures and two ways of life, which continues to this day.

Until the beginning of the sixteenth century, North America's indigenous people occupied the entire continent, with the only land disputes being those which arose between tribes. Indeed, on much of the continent, populations were scarce, and the lifestyles nomadic, so that the concept of ownership of the land was never an issue.

The arrival of Europeans resulted in localized conflict over rights to settle specific areas, but for nearly three centuries, there was always another ridgeline beyond which no European would go to settle, and the vast continent had enough space for the two cultures to coexist. By the beginning of the nineteenth century, 300 years of European immigration had brought the newcomers into enough of the continent so that the concept of large scale removal of the native population was raised as an issue.

*Right:* The Osage men Big Crow (Ko-ha-tunk-a), Bed Man (Nah-com-e-shee) and Not Afraid (Mun-ne-pus-kee).

By the beginning of the twentieth century, Native Americans no longer occupied the entire continent, but were relegated to specific, geographically-defined areas known in the United States as reservations and in Canada as reserves. Although implementation of the reservation as a definite policy was officially embraced by the United States in 1853, the idea itself can be traced to the United States government's long favored policy of concentrating the Native American population onto controlled expanses of land. By the end of the nineteenth century, the adoption of the reservation system represented the end of one era and the beginning of another.

According to the United States Bureau of Indian Affairs (BIA), "An Indian reservation is a specific area of land which has been reserved, set aside or acquired for the occupancy and use of an Indian tribe." In essence, a reservation is land a tribe reserved for itself when it relinquished its other land areas to the United States through treaties. The Bureau of Indian Affairs does not, however, run Native American reservations. Elected tribal governments oversee reservations, working with the Bureau of Indian Affairs whenever trust resources or bureau programs are involved.

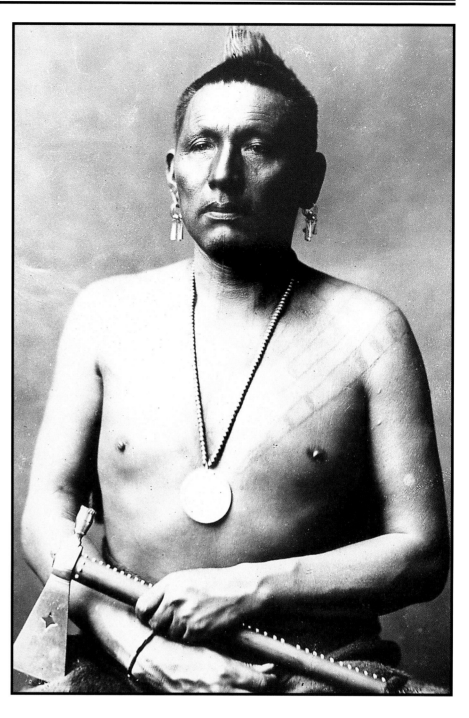

*Above:* Governor Pathinonpazhi of the Osage. Since the advent of the reservation system in the United States, many tribal leaders in the Southwest and elsewhere have adopted the title "governor."

The equivalent of the Bureau of Indian Affairs in Canada is the Department of Indian and Northern Affairs (DINA). Canadian Indians have banded together to form 633 First Nations communities throughout Canada. The Assembly of First Nations (formerly the National Indian Brotherhood) is a First Nations institution where the leaders of tribal governments assemble to devise common strategies on collective issues.

United States Census Bureau figures cite 1,959,234 American Indians and Alaska Natives as living in the United States in 1990 (1,878,285 American Indians, 57,152 Inuit (Eskimos), and 23,197 Aleuts). The Bureau of Indian Affairs' 1990 estimate is that almost 950,000 individuals of this total population live on or adjacent to federal Indian reservations. In Canada, data for the same time period shows a total of 533,189 native peoples, including 283,514 living on reserves.

A total of 56.2 million acres of land is currently held "in trust" by the United States for various Native American tribes and individuals. The majority of this is reservation land; however, not all reservation land is trust land. On behalf of the United States, the Secretary of the Interior serves as trustee for such lands, with many routine trustee responsibilities delegated to Bureau of Indian Affairs officials.

The number of Native American land areas in the United States administered as federal Indian reservations total 278, the vast majority of which are located in the western half of the United States. The government oversees reservations through the Bureau of Indian Affairs, which operates under the auspices of the Department of the Interior. Indian tribes that are "federally recognized" have a legal relationship with the United States government through treaties, acts of Congress, executive orders, or other administrative actions.

The annual budget for the Bureau of Indian Affairs has averaged approximately $1.5 billion. A typical fiscal year appropriation for the Bureau of Indian Affairs would be allocated to such program categories as education, $500 million; tribal services (including social services and law enforcement), $340 million; economic development, $15 million; natural resources, $140 mil-

*Below:* Women on the Navajo Reservation shearing sheep. Such livestock were an integral part of the Navajo economy during the reservation's first century.

lion; trust responsibilities, $75 million; facilities management, $95 million; general administration, $115 million; construction, $165 million; Indian loan guaranty, $12 million; and balance earmarked for miscellaneous payments to individual Native Americans, or specific one-time projects or allocations to special entities such as the Navajo Rehabilitation Trust Fund.

Under the Indian self-determination policy, tribes may operate their own reservation programs by contracting with the Bureau of Indian Affairs.

The largest reservation is the Navajo Reservation, which consists of some 16 million acres of land in Arizona, New Mexico and Utah.

Other large reservations include: Menominee in Wisconsin; Greater Leech Lake, White Earth and Red Lake in Minnesota; Fort Berthold and Fort Totten in North Dakota; Standing Rock (mostly in South Dakota), Cheyenne River, Crow Creek, Sisseton, Pine Ridge and Rosebud in South Dakota; Winnebago and Omaha in Nebraska; Osage in Oklahoma; Blackfeet, Fort Belknap, Fort Peck, Flathead and Crow in Montana; Wind River in Wyoming; Uintah and Ouray in Utah; Jicarilla, Mescalero and Canoncito in New Mexico; Hopi, San Carlos, Papago, Kaibab, Havasupai and Hualapai in Arizona; Fort Hall, Couer d'Alene and Nez Perce in Idaho; Colville, Spokane and Yakima in Washington; Warm Springs, Klamath and Umatilla in Oregon; and Western Shoshone, Pyramid Lake and Walker River in Nevada.

*Above, clockwise from top left:*
Four Wolves (Chah-ee-chopes),
Bear Den Woman (Oo-je-en-a-he-ha),
Red Bear (Duhk-pits-a-ho-shee) and
Two Crows (Pa-ris-ka-roo-pa).
All were members of the Osage tribe, met and
painted by George Catlin in the 1830s.

Many of the smaller reservations are less than 1,000 acres, with the smallest amounting to less than 100 acres. Smaller reservations are also called pueblos (mainly in New Mexico), rancheria (mainly in California) and communities. On each reservation, the local governing authority is the tribal government. The states in which the reservations are located have limited powers over them, and only as provided by federal law. On some reservations, however, a high percentage of the land is owned and occupied by non-Indians. Some 140 reservations have entirely tribally-owned land.

For many non-Indians reservations remain shrouded in mystery. Most whites have never set foot on a reservation. The Native American remains invisible, segregated, an enigma still.

*Above:* George Catlin's portraits of Dakota (Sioux) chiefs included Little Bear (Mah-to-tchee-ga) of the Hunkpapa band, and two views of The Dog (Shon-ka), the leader of the Caz-a-zshee-ta band.

Exposure to Indians comes from either cursory school discussions or television and movie westerns. Stereotypes of rural poverty still prevail. Indeed, reservation life can often be quite bleak, with high levels of alcoholism and high unemployment rates. These factors, combined with a low life expectancy rate have led many to compare reservations to Third World nations.

Recently, controversy has arisen over the issue of gaming, which is now legally sanctioned for reservations. Proponents of gaming argue that it generates much needed money for reservation economies, while opponents see the coming of organized gambling as a direct threat to Native American tradition. The debate continues.

The advent of the reservation system almost 150 years ago and its continuance as a way of life provides an important chapter in Native American history, one that has received little attention. Deprived of land that was rightfully theirs, the Indian was systematically forced to alter his lifestyle, culture and history. Some reservations were established on the land where Indians were already living. Others (such as the Cherokee, for example) were shuffled off their land in order to make way for the "new" country.

For people who believed in the holiness of their land and in the spiritual bond between the Creator and the Earth, the relocation was devastating. The reservation — both of yesterday and today — thus becomes a part of an enduring legacy of Native American struggle and survival.

# DEFINING NATIVE AMERICAN IDENTITY

Today, Native Americans present an interesting paradox. On the one hand, they share a common bond and have common interests and problems. On the other hand, they are a study in diversity, with individual tribes being separated by differences in language, customs and lifestyle. An Indian tribe can be generally defined as a cultural entity. Formed by a common history that often stretches back too far to measure, it is a group that shares the same race, religion, language, traditions and values.

What culture really means is that, as a result of sharing ways of life and experiences, the members of the group have common values. They look at the world in the same way and regard the same things as important. They make similar judgments and have a common definition of right and wrong.

The term "cultural entity" is a little vague and sometimes difficult to define. One might say, for example, that a single Hopi Indian village in Arizona is a "culture," different from other Hopi villages. Or one might say that all the Hopi people are a "culture," different from the Navajo, and that the Hopi and the Navajo together are a "culture," different from non-Indians. There are many ways to define a cultural entity.

Each Native American group is different from the other, but Indians share a common bond which may include such personal characteristics as a spiritual attachment to the land, a sharing with others, or a belief that a metaphysical power exists in all objects, animate and inanimate. Finally, a definition of Native Americans may include a desire to remain Indian and to retain their culture and language.

However, Indian tribes are something more than cultural entities. They also are political entities, and this makes them unique. In the United States, when members of other cultural entities have dealings with the federal government, they are seen as individuals dealing with a political entity. When a tribe has dealings with the United States, two political entities stand face-to-face and come to terms. Individual Native Americans are treated the way they are because they are members of a political entity, the tribe.

Thus a political entity is a group of people living within a certain territory under a government that has some sovereignty. Federally-recognized Indian tribes fall within this definition.

In the United States, federal recognition can mean a tribe has been acknowledged as having a government-to-government relationship with the United States. Federally recognized tribes are eligible to receive services from the Bureau of Indian Affairs and other federal agencies. Such recognition also may mean certain lands and natural resources of tribes fall under the dictates of the trust responsibility.

Congress, which may terminate tribes from federal recognition, may likewise restore tribes to the rolls and does so on occasion. The Secretary of the Interior also

*Right:* Rabbit Tail of the Shoshone was a scout who offered his services to white explorers, circa 1880.

may restore tribes to the rolls through the department's federal acknowledgment process.

An evaluation of each petition for recognition is made and a determination is handed down, stipulating whether or not the group or band meets the criteria to be recognized as a federal tribe. Some tribes, such as the Lumbee of North Carolina, a large tribe with many prominent members, have never had any relationship with the United States government.

As far as internal matters are concerned, tribes are self-governing. Unless specifically limited by treaty or act of Congress, Native American self-government generally includes the following areas:

- The right to adopt and operate under a form of government of their own choosing.
- The right to determine the requirements for membership.
- The right to regulate domestic relations of its members.
- The right to control the methods used in enacting municipal legislation.
- The right to administer justice.
- The right to levy taxes.
- The right to regulate the use of property within the territorial jurisdiction of the tribe.

*Above:* Sequoyah of the Cherokee is noted for having developed the first Native American phonetic alphabet. Developed in 1821, it had 85 characters. Sequoyah went to Indian Territory on the Trail of Tears and died there in 1843. This portrait by Charles Banks Wilson hangs in the Oklahoma state capitol.

Many tribes that have never been acknowledged have maintained some form of government and tribal customs, and some recognized tribes still have traditional forms of government. One such tribe is the Jemez Pueblo of New Mexico, which functions as a theocracy, with the religious leaders of the community selecting the pueblo's governor on a yearly basis. There are other New Mexico pueblos that operate their governments on a somewhat traditional basis.

The leaders of most tribes are called "chairmen." However, some are called "governor," and still others are called "president." Most tribal governing bodies are called "councils," but there is varying terminology, and some are called "business committee," or "general council" or "executive committee."

The present governments of many Indian tribes date back to the Indian Reorganization Act of 1934 (Wheeler-Howard Act) and have tribal constitutions patterned after the United States Constitution. Some tribes were organized under the Indian Reorganization Act and are called "IRA tribes," but have no constitutions.

The Eastern Band of Cherokee of North Carolina is an example of combining the old with the new. The Cherokee had a government and a tribal constitution before the Indian Reorganization Act was passed; then they were organized under the Indian Reorganization Act. Recently, they developed a more modern constitution. This document was then submitted to the tribal electorate in a referendum vote, before being sent to the office of the Secretary of Interior for approval.

Most of the Oklahoma and Kansas tribes, with the exception of the Osage, were excluded from the Indian Reorganization Act because they had no reservation lands. These tribes were organized under the Oklahoma Indian Welfare Act of 1936. The Osage were excluded from organizing under this act because they were operating under a special congressional act of 1906.

In Oklahoma, each of the four main groups of Creek, that form today's Creek Confederacy, has a tribal council with its seat of government at Okmulgee, Oklahoma. In 1970, Congress passed a law giving the Creek and other tribes in Oklahoma the right to popularly elect their principal officers. While the other

*Below:* A rare color photo of a pair of Blackfeet elders at a "pow-wow" at Browning, Montana on the Blackfeet Reservation, circa 1940. The man at the left is the noted chief, Bird Rattler.

four tribes designate their officers as "principal chiefs," the Chickasaw call their top official "governor." Most tribal officials, along with the tribe's legislative body, are elected for either two- or four-year terms.

The Navajo Nation has the United States' largest governing body, an 87-member tribal council elected every four years by popular vote of the electorate in 109 local Navajo chapters on the reservation. The chairman and vice chairman, who run as a team, are elected for corresponding terms. Either the chairman or the vice chairman is the presiding officer at meetings of the council, which meets four times annually, its sessions in accord with the seasons of the year.

Not all Native Americans live on reservations or reserves, but generally, tribes or tribal political authority is based on the reservation or reserve. As noted previously, an Indian reservation or Indian reserve can be defined as a specific area of land which has been set aside or acquired for the occupancy and use of an Indian tribe. Indian reservations come in every shape and size, ranging from a rancheria in California with less than one acre to a reservation with thousands of acres.

By creating reserves and reservations, the governments of both the United States and Canada had a number of ostensible purposes in mind; in addition, the reserve and the reservation has evolved and changed throughout their histories in North America. Initially functioning to reduce the land holdings of Native Americans, many reservations were subsequently established as places to relocate displaced Indians.

Tribes were shuffled westward in order to make room for the multiplying white settlers. In the most drastic scenarios, the reservation became a prison: Native Americans who resisted the westward expansion of the non-Indians were confined to boundaries dictated by the white man.

On the other hand, many reservations were set aside as sanctuaries, designed to protect Indians from non-Indians or from other tribes who were a direct threat to stability. More recently, reservations have been

*Below:* A Nez Perce man on horseback at the Nez Perce Reservation in eastern Oregon. The Nez Perce are noted for their Appaloosa horses.

*Above:* A healing ceremony at the Zia Pueblo in New Mexico, circa 1888. The boy in the foreground is receiving treatment from the shamans. The New Mexico pueblos, continuously inhabited for centuries, were designated as reservations by the Bureau of Indian Affairs.

acquired or set aside as a base for economic development or to provide housing sites.

In the United States, the earliest reservations were created by treaties, but later, many were set up by executive orders issued by the president. A large number have been designated by acts of Congress. Treaty reservations all predate 1871, at which time Congress prohibited further treaties with Indian tribes. Some reservations were created by a combination of these methods.

The power to set up executive order reservations was ended by Congress in 1919. Now, a reservation can be created — or expanded — only by a specific act of Congress or by the Secretary of the Interior, acting under the authority of the Indian Reorganization Act of 1934.

Though Native American tribes have governmental responsibilities and authorities on reservations, land on reservations can be owned by non-Indians. Many reservations do consist entirely of tribal land, but others have mixed ownership. In some instances, Congress opened reservation land areas to settlement by non-Indians and, in others, reservation land allotted to individual Indians was later conveyed to non-Indians. It is fairly common for the federal government to own some land on a reservation. Reservation land might also be owned by the state, or a political subdivision, a corporation or any private person.

The title to much of the Indian land existing today is held by the United States government as trustee for a Native American group, an individual Indian, or several individual Indians. Most individually owned trust land resulted directly or indirectly from the allotment process. The responsibilities which this trusteeship puts on the federal government are generally those specified by Congress in a complex pattern of laws as they are interpreted and applied by the executive branch of government and, more significantly, by the courts.

The question of who has jurisdiction on an Indian reservation is complicated and not easily answered in a few words. In general, several different governmental bodies may have jurisdiction for various purposes. Sometimes the jurisdiction may overlap. Also, a distinction needs to be made between jurisdiction over an area (territorial jurisdiction), jurisdiction over people and jurisdiction for certain legal purposes, (subject matter jurisdiction).

Indian tribes have all the elements of jurisdiction as an attribute of their sovereignty except insofar as that jurisdiction has been limited by Congress.

Often, jurisdictional issues are argued in the courts. A 1978 Supreme Court decision, Oliphant v. Suquamish Indian Tribe, held that Indian tribal courts do not have inherent criminal jurisdiction to try and punish non-Indians, and may not assume such jurisdiction unless specifically authorized by Congress.

Public Law 280 is a 1953 act of Congress which conferred jurisdiction on certain states over criminal offenses and civil causes of action committed or arising on Indian reservations.

An Indian may use allotted or fee land that belongs to him without getting approval from the Bureau of Indian Affairs or any other governmental agency. Tribal land is frequently used by members under so-called "assignments" without the necessity for any approval except from the tribe itself.

If an Indian desires to convey an interest in his land or encumber it or if he desires to exploit nonrenewable resources, such as minerals, he usually must have the approval of the Secretary of Interior.

*Above:* This 1868 portrait is of Betsy (Be-che), a member of the Omaha tribe who was a feminist and an early advocate of womens' rights on the reservation.

There is statutory authority for individual Native Americans to sell their trust land. This can be done only with Secretarial approval, and a finding must be made that the sale is in the owner's best interest.

Indians must obtain approval for most leases and all sales because Congress has imposed this requirement. Its purpose is to prevent people from taking advantage of the Native American and cheating him out of his land. In the approval process, the Bureau of Indian Affairs is required to determine that the lease or sale is fair to the Indian and is authorized by law.

Not all federally-recognized tribes have reservations. Oklahoma has mostly small reservations, but it has 1,207,573 acres of tribal trust land and individual lands held in trust by the United States government. Alaska's one reservation, the Annette Islands Reserve, is located on the southern tip of the Alaska panhandle. The 1,100 natives of the Annette Islands Reserve are Tlingit, Haida and Tsimshian. They elected to remain on a reservation when other Alaska Native reservations were abolished with the passage of the Alaska Native Claims Settlement Act in 1971.

*Below:* Betsy (Be-che) on horseback during the 1877 buffalo hunt. She was one of a handful of women who joined the men on the hunts.

*Above:*  Red Jacket (Sogoyewapha) was a gifted orator and an important leader of the Seneca people during the early part of the nineteenth century. Although he wore a British military coat — hence his English name — he fought with the Americans in the War of 1812. He died in 1830 and did not have to endure the indignity of exile to Indian Territory.

*Right:*  Indian Territory in 1891 was dominated by the areas assigned to the Cherokee, Creek, Choctaw and Chickasaw. The fifth of the "Civilized Tribes," the Seminole, originally shared space with the Creek, but got their own parcel in 1866. Other tribes were squeezed into the northeast corner. When Oklahoma Territory was formed in 1891, additional tribes had reservations there. In 1907, the entire area entered the union as the state of Oklahoma. Compare this map to the contemporary map of Oklahoma found on page 141.

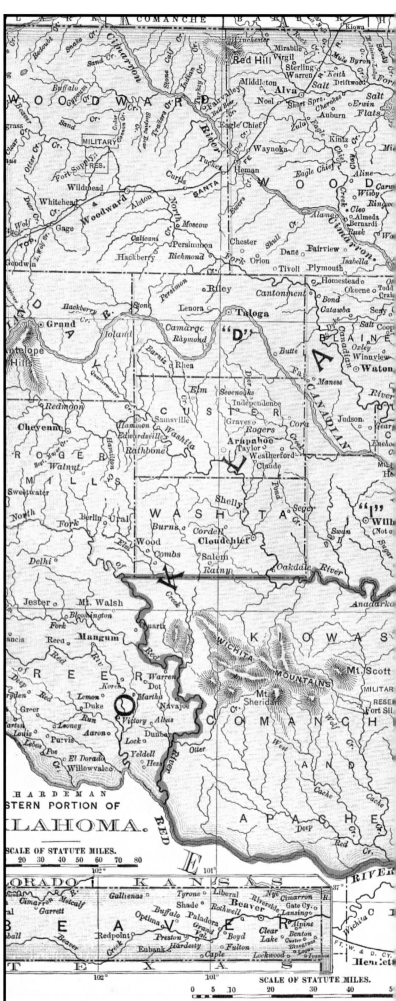

# IN THE BEGINNING

Of course, the beginning of Native American life and culture long predates contact with Europeans, but the history of reservations and reservation policy dates back to the first contact between these disparate cultures.

When Christopher Columbus made landfall at San Salvador on October 12, 1492, it was a milestone moment both for the European culture that the explorer and his crew represented, and for the indigenous native people of North America who greeted him there on that sandy shore. While Europeans and Native Americans had made contact with one another before, this time the Europeans had come to stay.

A century of ever-increasing European exploration on the North American continent led to the establishment of permanent settlements in what is now the United States and Canada. With the establishment of these settlements, the Europeans brought the widely-held notion that land claims could be made in the Western Hemisphere, regardless of the occupancy of the land by indigenous people already living there.

In the beginning, this arrangement was grudgingly accepted by the native population, so long as the European settlers confined themselves to relatively narrow strips of land near the coasts. As larger settlements began to develop, however, European and Native American interests came into conflict.

Early European contact with the Native Americans of America was based upon the belief that the Indians — like their European counterparts — were sovereign and independent nations. As the Old World rushed to settle in the New World, settlers and colonists found themselves faced with a difficult dilemma: what to do with the country's indigenous population — those that had been living in the area for centuries before their arrival?

During the course of the sixteenth century, the New World Columbus had "discovered" in 1492 was the object of a wave of European expeditions. Like Columbus himself, the first explorers were trying to find a way *around* the New World.

Magellan found the Southwest Passage around the tip of South America, and a great deal of expense was incurred and lives lost in the impossible effort to find a shorter, easier and more convenient Northwest Passage around the top of North America.

These efforts at navigation were soon joined by efforts at exploitation. After gold was discovered, the European conception of the New World went from being that of an obstacle to being that of a resource. The Spanish were lucky in that they found gold, and their outposts were set up largely to ship it back to their homeland. The English and French found little gold, but they began exploiting the abundant supply of beaver for their luxurious fur.

By the end of the sixteenth century, Europeans began to conceive of the New World as not so much a place to avoid or exploit, but as a place to put down

*Right:* During the 1870s, Chief Rain-in-the-Face was one of the most important leaders of the Hunkpapa Dakota (Sioux).

roots and *live*. With this, serious attempts at colonization began. North America was a harsh environment, and the earliest English and French attempts at colonization failed disastrously. Yet the people persisted, and by the beginning of the seventeenth century, permanent settlements began to take root.

In 1607, the English finally planted the seed that evolved into the largest English-speaking nation in the world. Captain John Smith founded his settlement at Jamestown (named for King James I) in the territory of Virginia, which was already inhabited by the Algonquian-speaking Powhatan people. King James I came to the throne of England in 1603. High on his list of priorities was the project of colonizing his American "possessions."

In April 1606, he issued two patents to men of his kingdom that authorized them to possess and colonize that portion of North America lying between the 34th and 45th parallels of latitude.

This territory, encompassing the area occupied by Algonquian-speaking Native Americans, extended from the Cape Fear River in present North Carolina to Passamaquoddy Bay between what are now Maine and New Brunswick. The first patent was directed to nobles, gentlemen and merchants residing in London.

Their corporation was called The London Company, and its primary motivation was colonization and commerce. The second patent was granted to a like body of men who comprised The Plymouth Company, which was located in Plymouth. The Plymouth Company authorized settlement in their area by a religious movement called Puritans, who arrived off the coast of what is now Massachusetts in December 1620.

The immigrants survived the snows of winter to establish their colony. Soon after, Samoset, a leader of the Wampanoag tribe, came into the Plymouth colony, offered his hand, and welcomed the strangers. He could speak some English, because he'd been with the Europeans at intervals since the time of the earlier voyages. He told them of his people and of a great plague that had killed many people a few years earlier.

A short time later, another Native American named Squanto, who had been to England and learned to speak English, visited Plymouth and confirmed what Samoset had said. Later in the spring, the colonists were introduced to Massasoit, the great chief of the Wampanoag, and with him they entered into a treaty that remained in place for half a century.

The agreement simply provided that no injury would be done by the Europeans to Native Americans or by Native Americans to the European settlers, and that all offenders should be given up by either party for punishment according to the laws of the two peoples. Later, nine of the other leading tribes entered into similar pacts with the English. Though there would continue to be difficult times for the Plymouth colony, its third year,

*Above:* When Columbus returned to Spain after his first voyage, he brought with him, a number of Native Americans. They were treated with curiosity, but regarded more as "specimens" than as representatives of a distinct culture.

1623, brought a plentiful harvest, and the people of Plymouth began to share their agricultural products with the Native Americans, who brought wild game to exchange for corn.

An important figure in relations between Europeans and the native populations in New England during the seventeenth century was Roger Williams, a Salem clergyman who had ironically been banished from Plymouth due to his religious views, even though they embodied the true principles of religious liberty on which the parent colony was founded. He was embraced by the Native Americans, whose rights he had defended, and was entertained by Massasoit of the Wampanoag and Canonicum of the Narragansett. In 1636, he and his followers put down roots in a place they named Providence. No man of the period, nor possibly in the history of New England, deserves more enduring fame — not so much for what he did in the founding of a successful colony, but for his relations with Native Americans.

The Narragansett and Pequot were hereditary enemies, but through the persuasion of Williams, they became reconciled and made a treaty of friendship with the English. The détente was short-lived, however, for the Pequot both feared and distrusted the English.

They formed an alliance with the Narragansett and Mohegan, whom they persuaded to join them in a war. When the situation became critical, Williams notified Sir Henry Vane, the governor of Massachusetts, of the peril. He then went alone to the Narragansett camp, where he successfully pleaded with leaders to stand by their vows of peace.

By the 1670s, however, relations between the colonists and the Native Americans began to deteriorate. This resulted in the conflict known as King Philip's War, named for the Wampanoag chief, Metacomet, who was known to the settlers as "King Philip."

The catalyst for the conflict came when a Native American who was on intimate terms with the Europeans was murdered by three Native Americans. They were apprehended and brought to trial before a jury of Europeans and Native Americans. They were convicted and shot, an incident that precipitated the war that had been expected for some time. Metacomet assembled his warriors and took up a position in the woods near where the city of Bristol now stands.

In June 1675, a group of people returning from church in Swansea were fired upon by Native Americans, who killed three settlers and burned barns and cabins. Several villages were then attacked by the Native Americans. Soon all of Plymouth colony was involved. Members of the Nipmuck tribe joined the fray in August, and Brookfield became the scene of a conflict. The struggle continued for nearly a year with great loss of life and property on both sides. Metacomet himself was killed near his old home at Mount Hope in Rhode Island.

*Above:* Dutch traders involved in negotiations with representatives of the Iroquois people over issues related to trade and land use, circa 1640.

Meanwhile, the French obtained a footing in Nova Scotia and on the banks of the St. Lawrence River in an area populated by the Iroquoian-speaking Native Americans. In 1623, French explorer Etienne Brule became the first European to see Lake Superior, not only the largest of the Great Lakes, but also the largest body of fresh water on Earth. With the trappers and traders came the priests, who saw their goal as bringing the message of Christianity to the Native Americans. By mid-century, French trading posts and missions could be found in what are now Michigan, Ontario and Wisconsin.

Although the French made a general claim of sovereignty over the lands of the interior, they did little to disturb the Native American possession of them aside from establishing small forts and trading posts. The fur trade with the Indians dominated the economy and much of the daily activity.

It should be pointed out that at this time the tribes of the Iroquois Confederacy — the Mohawk, Oneida, Onondaga, Cayuga and Seneca — were the dominant non-European political force on the southern side of the St. Lawrence. On the northern side, the dominant tribe was the Huron people, who were also Iroquoian-speakers. English and French interests came to blows in the Ohio River Valley, which stretches nearly a thousand miles from the Appalachian Mountains to the Mississippi River. England and France each believed this land belonged to them through discovery, exploration, early settlement, long-standing

*Below:* Native Americans presenting hides to Dutch traders. Well into the seventeenth century, the trading relationship between the Europeans and the Native Americans continued to be mutually beneficial.

treaties, royal grants and purchase from various Native American tribes.

To the English, particularly the colonists of Pennsylvania and Virginia, as well as members of The Ohio Company, the Ohio country was a natural area for expansion by trade and settlement. The French saw it as an economic and defensive link between their colonies of Canada and Louisiana, as well as a buffer to English movements beyond the Appalachians.

Both nations aggressively sought the goodwill and assistance of the Algonquian- and Iroquoian-speaking Native American

*Above:* Eighteenth century confrontations between settlers and Native Americans were greatly feared by the former. As this nineteenth century lithograph clearly shows, the settlers were portrayed as heroic, and the Native Americans as savage.

residents through propaganda and presents distributed by traders and agents. The Native Americans' concept of land ownership conflicted with European values and culture, and this contributed to their claims to the territory being ignored or forgotten. The French used Native Americans such as the Algonquian-speaking Shawnee people to harass and hold back English attempts to trade or settle in the area. Other tribes, including many of the Iroquois Confederacy, assisted the English. The defeat of the French in the war of 1755-1763 led to the ascendancy of the English colonies as political units. Within a generation, they would revolt against England itself and form the United States.

The Articles of Confederation, approved in 1777 but not made effective until 1781, introduced one of the many contradictory elements found in Native American affairs.

What the Confederation did was divide responsibility for Native American affairs between the central government and the states. At the same time, it agreed in principle that the central government should regulate Native American affairs and manage Indian trade. The notion of giving the 13 original states responsibility for Indians residing within their boundaries and investing in the central government responsibility for all other Indians strengthened the concept of "Indian Country," but it perplexed many people. President James Madison, writing in *The Federalist*, called it "absolutely incomprehensible" and likened it to subverting a mathematical axiom, "by taking away a part, and letting the whole remain."

The framers of the United States Constitution attempted to eliminate the problem by calling for specific constitutional authority for federal supervision of Native Americans in the Commerce Clause. Provisions for making treaties with Native Americans were established, and Congress was charged with the responsibility "to regulate commerce with foreign nations, and among the several States and with the Indian tribes."

Moreover, it stipulated that the Constitution and all treaties (including treaties with Indian tribes) ". . . shall be the supreme law of the land . . . anything in the Constitution or laws of any State to the contrary notwithstanding." Some years later, Chief Justice John Marshall, in Worcester v. Georgia, made it clear that the Constitution confers on the national government "all that is required for the regulation of our intercourse with the Indians. They are not limited by any restrictions on their free actions; the shackles imposed on this power, in the Confederation, are discarded."

Courts have consistently reaffirmed these powers of the central government. In practice, however, the 13 original states maintained supervision over Native Americans within their boundaries. The division of authority established in the Articles of Confederation spawned numerous complex legal problems, some of which are still being considered by the courts today.

In grouping Indian tribes with states and foreign nations in the Commerce Clause, the United States was recognizing the Native Americans as a separate and distinct political entity to be dealt with on a government-to-government basis.

In 1778, the first treaty was signed between an Indian tribe, the Delaware, and the newly-formed United States government. In signing this treaty, the United States was following the English and European tradition of dealing with tribes as political entities.

Early United States policy thus remained consistent with the European practice of recognizing tribes as governments with full internal sovereignty. At one point it was even expected that certain tribes would be organized into states and one day be granted representation in Congress.

In the early 1830s, Chief Justice Marshall further reaffirmed the nature of Indian tribes as sovereigns in Cherokee Nation v. Georgia and Worcester v. Georgia. The high court decisions characterized Indian tribes as dependent sovereign nations possessing all attributes of sovereignty save those which Congress has expressly limited or taken away.

Subject to some judicial and legislative amendments, the conclusions reached in these cases concerning the status and sovereignty of tribes have survived to the present day.

Marshall used the phrase "domestic dependent nations" to describe the political status of tribes. These words were a way of expressing the fact that tribes, after conquest and through treaty, had agreed to regard themselves as under the protection of the United States.

Marshall's definition acknowledged two ways in which tribal sovereignty, by 1832, had been limited. First, by accepting the protection of the United States, tribes agreed to extinguish their external sovereignty. Second, by treaties, and again as protected nations, tribes agreed to recognize the legislative powers of Congress over them. This second limitation is commonly referred to as "plenary," which means absolute or total. It should be noted, however, that even this process has its roots in mutual agreement. The tribes had consented in treaties to give Congress this power.

Also, this agreement did not extinguish tribal sovereignty. A tribe's sovereign powers can be removed only by specific, positive acts, and they can be removed only by the federal government. Powers not removed remain sovereign powers — inherent, not given.

Over the years, however, that "sovereignty" would steadily erode. Tribes were not left alone as promised. As westward expansion continued and the Native American was either vilified as a heathen or romanticized as a noble savage, it became obvious that the government would have to "deal" with the people already

*Above:* Virginia's John Marshall served as the chief justice of the United States Supreme Court from 1801 until his death in 1835. He defined Native American tribes as nations under the protection of the United States and not truly sovereign.

living there. The land they lived upon was desperately needed. The country was rapidly growing, and the concept of herding the Native Americans away quickly gained favor among government leaders, although thought of where exactly to send the Native Americans was not so clearly defined. No longer did the Native Americans have the freedom and sovereignty to live as they wished. The government expected them to make way for the white man's progress.

The treaties continued (370 in all, spanning the years from 1778 to 1871), most of which ceded Native American lands to the government. Promises made to the various tribes (such as assurances that no more land would be taken, and that food and supplies would be forthcoming) were often broken or ignored. It became apparent that the Native Americans would neither be assimilated into white culture nor give up their land.

Supported by President Andrew Jackson, the Indian Removal Act of 1830 sought to relocate all Indians living east of the Mississippi River.

When the United States government began enforcement of the act, its practitioners asserted that a separate Indian Territory was the only sensible answer. The Indians, of course, had no say in the matter. In 1853, after years of broken promises, faulty treaties, policy reversals, inconsistencies and a government sanctioned policy of Indian "removal," the United States came up with another solution: the reservation.

*Below:* The Iroquois and Algonquin people had been at war with one another for centuries before the arrival of the Europeans. It was seen as being to a tribe's advantage to ally itself with such a heavily armed European force. In the war of 1755-1763 — known as the French and Indian War — the Algonquin tribes allied themselves with the French, while the Iroquois aided the British.

# THE INDIAN REMOVAL ACT

Early in the nineteenth century, discussion began on a proposed plan that would move all Native Americans west of the Mississippi. President Thomas Jefferson, who had serious doubts about the constitutionality of the Louisiana Purchase, regarded this plan as partial justification for the cession. For this reason, the landmark 1804 act which organized the new territory also authorized the president to exchange Native American lands east of the river for land to the west.

Under this authority, some tribes were moved. However, it was not until the 1820s and the presidency of James Monroe that the policy of removal and the establishment of separate government-designated Native American land gained momentum. Official adoption came with the passage of the Indian Removal Act in 1830. Determining the significance of the Indian Removal Act is essential for a comprehensive understanding of what eventually would banish the Indian to the reservation system. Mounting pressure came from citizens of states and territories with rapidly growing populations. They demanded further cession of native lands, preferring an outright expulsion of all Native Americans from within their borders. States and territories to the west of these states not only demanded the same policy but additionally did not want to be the homeland for the displaced Indians.

The government needed to take action on what was increasingly becoming the Indian "problem" — that is, the joint problems of:

1. What to do with Indians living on desirable land.
2. What to do with this population once they have been removed.

Passing by a close vote in the House of Representatives in May 1830, the Indian Removal Act sought to transport all Indians east of the Mississippi to a place designated as "Permanent Indian Country." The area in which the displaced Indians would live included land west of Arkansas and Missouri, as well as a line running through western Iowa, central Minnesota, and northwestern Wisconsin.

President Andrew Jackson, who had long opposed treating tribes as independent entities and who favored removal, enthusiastically executed the measure, and (with the exception of the Quakers) the act enjoyed widespread popular support in the United States. As Jackson delicately phrased it in his Seventh Annual Message to Congress on December 7, 1835, the act made "arrangements for the physical comfort and for the moral improvement of the Indians." Opponents of Jackson and removal believed that the federal government was obligated through treaty, legislation and custom to recognize tribal title to native lands and the right of Native Americans to self-government of tribes. As long as a tribe had not yet surrendered its title to certain

*Right:* John Ross, the eminent Cherokee leader, fought Indian "removal" in court, but his appeals were ignored.

*Left:* The Thinker (Not-o-way) was a member of the Seneca tribe of the Iroquois confederacy who was interviewed by George Catlin late in the 1830s.

*Above:* Old Bear (Mah-to-he-hah) was a Mandan shaman encountered by George Catlin during an expedition to the upper Missouri River country.

lands, then that tribe was guaranteed by treaty to be able to continue living there.

On the other hand, supporters of Jackson and removal considered treaties to be nothing more than convenient devices that obtained lands already under the sovereignty of the United States. As Georgia governor George Gilmer put it at the time: "Treaties were expedients by which ignorant, intractable, and savage people were induced without bloodshed to yield up what civilized people had the right to possess by virtue of that command of the Creator delivered to man upon his formation — be fruitful, multiply, and replenish the earth, and subdue it."

Because treaties had already dispossessed most of the northeastern tribes of their tribal homes, they offered little resistance. The only exception was the brief Black Hawk War of 1832, which involved a faction of the Sac and Fox under Chief Black Hawk. Among the northern tribes removed were the Chippewa, Winnebago, Potawatomi, Iowa, Kickapoo, Delaware, Shawnee, Ottawa, Kaskaskia, Peoria, and the Miami. In the south, however, there was considerable resistance. Five southern tribes — the Creek, Cherokee, Choctaw, Chickasaw, and Seminole — had come to be known as The Five Civilized Tribes because they adopted the customs of the white settlers around them. The Creek and the Cherokee, for instance, had established permanent homes and farms, in addition to setting up a form of representative government. The removal of the southern tribes (most significantly, the Seminole, who had been living in Florida for generations) began with threats, and eventually led to force. The resulting Seminole Wars (1835-1842) cost approximately 1,500 lives and $10 million. Finally, all but a small fraction of this Florida tribe were transported west. The task of moving 60,000 Native Americans to their new homes proved to be extremely difficult.

The Indian Removal Act's impact on the Cherokee Nation was — like that of other tribes — devastating. About 200 years ago the Cherokee were one tribe, or "Indian Nation," that lived in the southeast part of what is now the United States. During the period of the Indian Removal Act, many Cherokee were moved west to a territory that is now Oklahoma. A number remained in the southeast and gathered in North Carolina, where they purchased land and continued to live. Others went into the Appalachian Mountains to escape relocation. Many of their descendants may still live there now.

The eventual migration west would be a painful and laborious process. With their farms and towns, the Cherokee were by no means nomadic. John Ross, a Cherokee leader, wanted to fight removal through the courts. On the other hand, another leader, John Ridge, told his people to accept the inevitability of moving west: reversal of the act was futile. Many Cherokee families planned to hide in the surrounding caves and foothills, while others simply gave up and headed west.

Court action did manage to slow down the Cherokee's removal. Among the few who spoke out against the removal of the Cherokee and other tribes was Tennessee Senator Davy Crockett. As the court cases went on, the Georgia government was selling 160-acre plots of farmland and 40-acre mining sites. The land was needed and the Cherokee were, quite simply, in the way. Between 1790 and 1830 the population of Georgia increased sixfold. The western push of the settlers created a problem. Georgians continued to take Native American lands and force them into the frontier. A song was even created by the settlers waiting for the Cherokee to be removed: "All I want in this creation/Is a pretty little wife and a big plantation/Way down yonder in the Cherokee Nation."

While the Cherokee were fighting for the right to stay on their land, most of the other Indian nations had already succumbed to the enforcement of the act.

In 1835 a working treaty was made between the Cherokee and the United States. The terms of the agreement included the forfeiture of current lands for new land in the West, plus a cash settlement. Cherokee leader Lewis Cass cried foul, claiming that only five percent of the Cherokee population actually signed the bill and that bribery might have been involved. Ridge was believed to be bribed into accepting the treaty. A congressional committee was set up to investigate the fraud, but the treaty was

*Above:* Traders and Native Americans often got along well on the frontier, but when settlers came to establish farms and towns, the two cultures came to blows and the settlers asked the government to "remove" the previous residents.

eventually ratified. Ross did petition against the treaty, but the appeal was ignored. Deportation was to start in October, 1838.

What ensued is one of the most tragic episodes in American history. Although Georgia had been their home for generations, men, women and children were taken from their land, herded into makeshift forts with minimal facilities and food, and then forced to march a thousand miles. Under the generally indifferent army commanders, human losses for the first groups of Cherokee removed were extremely high. John Ross made an urgent appeal to Washington to let him lead his tribe west and the federal government agreed.

Ross organized the Cherokee into smaller groups and let them move separately through the wilderness so they could forage for food. The parties under Ross left in early fall and arrived in what is now Oklahoma (but which was then designated as Indian Territory) during the brutal winter of 1838-1839. Ross was able to significantly reduce the loss of life among his people. However, approximately 4,000 Cherokee died as a result of the removal. The route they traversed and the journey itself became known as "The Trail of Tears" or (to cite the direct Cherokee translation) "The Trail Where They Cried."

*Below:* The Native Americans who were forced to move to Oklahoma attempted to reestablish some semblance of their former lifestyle. The climate was much harsher and it would be many years before they had fully adapted.

# RESISTANCE AND RESERVATION

The removal called for in the Indian Removal Act was all but complete by 1837. A total of 94 treaties were signed between the Indians and the United States government, stipulating that according to law and treaty the Indians would be entitled to live in "Permanent Indian Country" for "as long as grass shall grow and water run."

The promise was quickly and habitually broken. The American westward movement soon began in earnest, and a decade later, it pushed through what was supposed to be the "Permanent Indian Country."

Slowly Native American land was ceded to the government. Beginning in 1851, a series of Fort Laramie treaties were signed with the Dakota (Sioux), Cheyenne, Arapaho and other Plains tribes. The pacts delineated the extent of their territories and allowed passage across these territories in exchange for payments to the tribes. Thus began the incursions of miners and wagon trains on the Oregon and later the Bozeman trails, few at first but an onslaught after the end of the Civil War.

During the 1850s, various Plains tribes were moved from Kansas and Nebraska into the new Indian Territory (now Oklahoma). In addition, the Homestead Act of 1862 unleashed a flood of settlers upon Native American lands. The idea of a "Permanent Indian Country" was officially abandoned in 1868, in favor of the reservation system.

It became obvious that the United States government had to create a federal agency to adequately deal with its policy toward Indians, which was becoming increasingly problematic. Thus, in 1834, the Bureau of Indian Affairs (BIA) was established by the Secretary of War.

The Bureau of Indian Affairs received official recognition from Congress in 1834 and remained under the auspices of the War Department until the passing of a congressional act on March 3, 1849. The act established the Home Department of the Interior, and thus the government's handling of Indian affairs passed from military to civilian control.

During the nineteenth century, the organizational structure of the Bureau of Indian Affairs had two types of field jurisdictions: superintendents and agents. The superintendents were primarily responsible for Indian affairs within a geographical area, usually a territory. Agents (some of whom reported to superintendents, while others reported directly to the Indian affairs office) were concerned with the affairs of one or more tribes.

As the settlers continued to force their way westward, another form of removal was incorporated into treaties made with tribes: establishment of reservations. Mention of the reservation as a solution to the Indian problem first surfaced in 1853. The earliest reservations were created by treaties. Later, many were set up either through an executive order issued by the president or through acts of Congress.

*Right:* In 1832, Chief Keokuk was recognized by Andrew Jackson as the leader of the Sac tribe.

By the 1840s, most Indian tribes had been removed from the Eastern half of the country to land west of the Mississippi. However, the enlarged boundaries of the United States, combined with the increasing numbers of white settlers in the West, transferred many of the same issues to the trans-Mississippi West. Under the expansionist policies of President James K. Polk, tribes in the Southwest, California, Northwest and Plains areas suddenly found themselves under American jurisdiction and policy. Treaties negotiated during the 1840s and 1850s with Native Americans living in these locations comprised the second phase of removal.

The campaign to subdue the "wild" Indians of the Plains began in full force. In 1849, the Commissioner of Indian Affairs made the proposition that Plains Indians should live upon limited reservations with distinct boundaries. The Native Americans

*Below:* A pair of young Wichita women photographed in 1870.

would be forbidden to travel beyond certain areas, and would also become "civilized." As interest in a transcontinental railroad escalated in the early 1850s, the Indians were once again "in the way." Tribes previously taken from their home in the East to supposedly permanent homes in what is now Kansas and Nebraska now were forced to move for a second time. In the meantime, skirmishes continued between the United States Army and those Indians resisting their internment to reservations.

In the late fall of 1865, nine treaties were signed with the Dakota (Sioux) people. Although these treaties were widely advertised as signifying the end of the Plains wars, none of the war chiefs had actually signed any of the treaties. Then, in the late spring of 1866, war chiefs Red Cloud, Spotted Tail, Standing Elk, Dull Knife and others came to Fort Laramie to negotiate a treaty concerning access to the Powder River Basin in Wyoming and Montana.

Shortly after the talks had begun on June 13, Colonel Henry Carrington and several hundred infantrymen reached Fort Laramie to build forts along the Bozeman trail. It was clear to the chiefs that the treaty was a mere formality. The road would be opened

*Above:* A Pawnee village photographed near Loup, Nebraska by William Henry Jackson in 1873.

whether they agreed or not. This was the beginning of Red Cloud's War, a series of triumphs for the great Dakota leader of the same name.

It was not until two years later, in the Treaty of 1868, that the Army agreed to abandon the forts on the Bozeman Trail. The treaty also created the Great Sioux Reservation and stated that the Sioux would not cede their hunting grounds in Montana and Wyoming territories. The Indians agreed to become "civilized."

In 1867 and 1868, the Indian Peace Commission negotiated the last of the 370 treaties made between tribes and the United States. These final treaties required tribes of the upper Great Plains, the Southwest and the Northwest to settle on various reservations. The last treaty, entered into with the Nez Perce of the Pacific Northwest on August 13, 1868, removed the tribe to a reservation in Idaho.

Resistance was perhaps futile, but many Western and Plains Indians fought their subjection. Throughout the 1870s, various outbreaks occurred, specifically on the southern Plains in 1874, in Dakota Territory in 1876 and in Montana in 1878.

The famous "Centennial Campaign" of 1876 — which climaxed with the defeat of Colonel George Armstrong Custer's 7th Cavalry in the Battle of the Little Bighorn — was launched by General Philip Sheridan, specifically to force the Dakota (Sioux) and Northern Cheyenne people back to the reservations from which they had strayed in an effort to return to traditional hunting grounds. Dakota Chief Sitting Bull had organized the greatest gathering of Native Americans on the northern Plains and it was this encampment that Custer charged. His detachment of just over 200 cavalrymen was easily beaten by over 2,500 Dakota and Northern Cheyenne warriors.

The defeat led to an outcry of public opinion in favor of using military force to keep the Indians on the reservations to which they'd been assigned. In October, General Nelson "Bear Coat" Miles arrived at Yellowstone River in order to take command of the campaign against the northern Plains Indians. The United States government issued an ultimatum that all Sioux who were not on the Great Sioux Reservation by January 31 would be considered hostile. The winter, however, was bitter and most Sioux did not even hear of the ultimatum until after the deadline.

In 1878, the Cheyenne attempted to live elsewhere besides the reservation assigned to them. In January of that same year, a commission found the Indian Bureau permeated with "cupidity, inefficiency, and the most barefaced dishonesty." The department's affairs were "a reproach to the whole nation."

Along with the Sioux and other Plains Indians, one of the last holdouts was the famed Nez Perce leader Chief Joseph, who finally surrendered to the government in 1877. The Nez Perce were a people living in a region extending from Idaho to Northern Washington. The tribe had maintained good relations with white people from the time of the Lewis and Clark expedition, and Joseph himself had spent much of his early childhood at a mission maintained by Christian missionaries.

The treaty history of relations between the Nez Perce and the United States government was typical of the experiences of other tribes. In 1855, Chief Joseph's father had signed a treaty with the United States that allowed his people to retain much of their traditional land. In 1863, another treaty was created that severely reduced the amount of Nez Perce land, but Joseph's father, Old Joseph, maintained that this second treaty was never agreed to by his people. A showdown over the issue came after Chief Joseph assumed his role as chief in 1877. It was determined that the Nez Perce would be moved from Oregon to Idaho, and General Oliver Howard reported that they had agreed to go, not willingly, but under constraint. Some whites were killed, and Chief White Bird sent word that he would not leave, whereupon an unequal war began between retreating bands of Nez Perce and companies of United States cavalry, aided by volunteers.

*Right:* This 1891 map of South Dakota shows the important Indian reservations which existed there at that time. The Pine Ridge and Rosebud reservations would see serious confrontations.

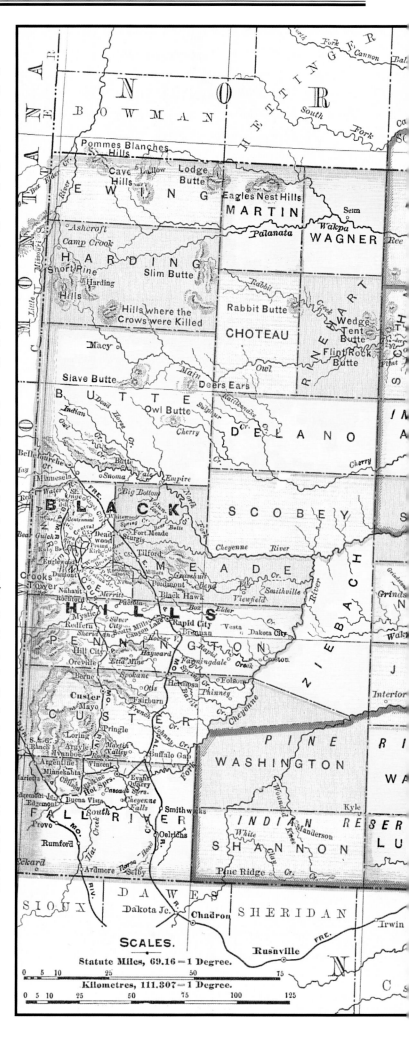

The Indians crossed the Yellowstone Park and River, endeavoring to escape into British territory, but were followed closely by Howard, and headed off by General (then Colonel) Nelson Miles. In the battle that ensued near the mouth of Eagle Creek, six chiefs and 25 warriors were killed, and 38 men wounded. Two officers and 21 men were killed, and four officers and 38 men wounded, on the side of the pursuers. The whole camp of about 450 men, women, and children fell into Colonel Miles's hands. Howard reached the battlefield just in time to be present at the surrender. Chief Joseph conducted this retreat with very extraordinary skill. He beat Colonel Gibbon with 15 officers, 146 troopers, and 34 volunteers, though he suffered severe losses. He stampeded the cavalry horses and pack-train, fought Colonel Sturgis on the Yellowstone River, where he lost many horses. However, he successfully eluded being captured by the troops.

Of this campaign, General William Tecumseh Sherman said: "The Indians throughout displayed a courage and skill that elicited universal praise; they abstained from scalping; let captive women go free; did not commit indiscriminate murder of peaceful families, which is usual; and fought with almost scientific skill."

*Above:* Chief Joseph of the Nez Perce was a respected leader, and a gifted orator. His real name was Hinmaton Yalatkit.

Joseph attempted to reach the Canadian border, but the Nez Perce supplies and will to fight on finally came to an end on the snowy plains of northern Montana. Tired of fighting, tired of resisting, a weary Chief Joseph declared, "Hear me, my chiefs, my heart is sick and sad. From where the sun now stands I will fight no more against the white man."

After months of fighting and forced marches, many of the Nez Perce were sent to a reservation in what is now Oklahoma, where many died from malaria and starvation. Chief Joseph tried every possible appeal to the federal authorities to return the Nez Perce to the land of their ancestors. In 1885, he was sent, along with many of his band, to a reservation in Washington where, according to the reservation doctor, he later died of a broken heart. Joseph is also recorded to have said, "If the white man wants to live in peace with the Indian we can live in peace. There need be no trouble. Treat all men alike. Give them all the same law. Give them all an even chance to live and grow. You might as well expect the rivers to run backward as that any man who is born a free man should be contented when penned up and denied liberty to go where he pleases. We ask only for an even chance to live as other men live. We ask to be recognized as men. Let me be a free man. . . free to travel. . . free to stop. . . free to work. . . free to choose my own teachers. . . free to follow the religion of my Fathers. . . free to think and talk and act for myself."

The situation with the Plains Indians continued to worsen. According to government documents, the Native Americans assuming the most threatening attitude of hostility were the Cheyenne and the Dakota, who were then identified as Sioux.

For several years following their subjugation in 1877, 1878, and 1879, "the most dangerous element" of the Cheyenne and the Sioux were placed under military control. Many of them were disarmed and dismounted; their war ponies were sold and the proceeds returned to them in domestic stock, farming utensils and wagons.

Many of the Cheyenne, under the charge of military officers, were located on land in accordance with the laws of Congress, but

*Below:* Nez Perce women doing their laundry in a stream on the Nez Perce Reservation in Oregon, circa 1920.

after they were turned over to civil agents and the vast herds of buffalo and large game had been destroyed, their supplies were insufficient. They were forced to kill cattle belonging to nearby white settlers.

The Manypenny Commission demanded that the Sioux give up an area known as Paha Sapa or starve. Having no choice, Red Cloud, Spotted Tail and the other reservation chiefs were forced to yield Paha Sapa. On May 7, 1877, a small band of Minneconjou Sioux was defeated by Miles, thus ending the Great Sioux Wars.

About this time several famed Native American leaders either fled or surrendered. In early May 1877 Crazy Horse surrendered at Fort Robinson and Sitting Bull escaped to Canada, along with approximately 300 followers. Eventually, on July 19, 1881, Sitting Bull and 186 of his remaining followers surrendered at Fort Buford. Sitting Bull was sent to Fort Randall for two years as a prisoner of war instead of being pardoned, as promised. In the Southwest, the Apache chief Geronimo held out against the US Army until 1886.

By the turn of the decade conditions were ripe for rebellion. Extreme poverty and lack of food, as well as the usual broken promises and an escalation of mistrust and misunderstanding, resulted in the Sioux outbreak of 1890. Only a year before, in 1889, the Sioux had signed an agreement with the United States government which broke up the Great Sioux Reservation. The Sioux would get six separate small reservations instead. The major part of their land was thus thrown open to settlers.

According to a telegram from General Miles to Senator Henry Dawes before the skirmish, "The Indians were urged and almost forced to sign a treaty presented to them by the commission authorized by Congress, in which they gave up a valuable portion of their reservation which is now occupied by white people. The government has failed to fulfill its part of the compact, and instead of an increase or even a reasonable supply for their support, they have been compelled to live on half and two-thirds rations, and received nothing for the surrender of their lands; neither has the government given any positive assurance that they intend to do any differently with them in the future."

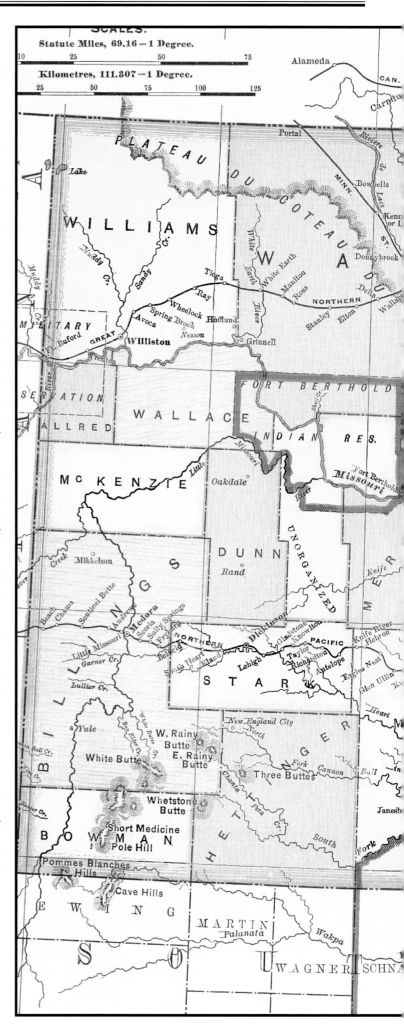

*Right:* This map shows the reservations that existed in North Dakota in 1891. Less area of the state was devoted to reservations than in South Dakota.

Drought, crop failure and the lack of adequate food all contributed to the Sioux's mounting frustration. Government agents and officers admitted that the Indians had not been receiving sufficient rations as stipulated by previous treaties. The majority of the Sioux were under the charge of civil agents, who were frequently changed and often inexperienced. Many of the tribes became rearmed and remounted. They claimed that the government had not fulfilled its treaties and had failed to make large enough appropriations for their support. Others gave up. The poor living conditions were so serious that thousands left the area, either going over the mountains to the Pacific slope or returning to the area east of the Missouri or the Mississippi rivers.

Such despair fostered not only physical resistance but also spiritual resistance, as evidenced by the rise of revivalist religious movements such as the Shaker religion of the Northwest (1881) and the Ghost Dance (1890). The Ghost Dance movement was begun by Wovoka, a Paiute shaman from Nevada, who preached that all white people were about to be swept out of North America and all of the buffalo — whose numbers had been reduced from millions to a few thousand in the preceding decades — returned.

Wovoka's new religion particularly caught fire on the Sioux reservation, where it promised a return to the Native American's vanishing way of life. These last glimmers of a return to the past and the old ways were, however, short-lived. Both movements were eventually subsumed by the reservation, which was to become the permanent "home" for the Indian. The government's idea of "Permanent Indian Country" was finally realized.

The massacre at the South Dakota hamlet of Wounded Knee in 1890 marked the end of serious resistance to confinement on reservations. Along with The Trail of Tears, the Wounded Knee Massacre stands out as one of the most infamous events in Indian history. On a December morning in 1890, soldiers opened fire on a group of unarmed Indians (120 men, 230 women and children) who had earlier agreed to surrender and relocate to Pine Ridge reservation. One figure estimates that close to 300 of the 350 Indians lay dead or crawled away, only to die afterward.

One eyewitness, American Horse, provides a chilling account of the day's horrors: "There was a woman with an infant in her arms who was killed as she almost touched the flag of truce, and the women and children of course were strewn all along the

*Above:* Spotted Tail (Tshin-tah-las-kah), the great Brule Dakota (Sioux) chief, was photographed in 1872 by Alexander Gardner.

circular village until they were dispatched. Right near the flag of truce a mother was shot down with her infant; the child not knowing that its mother was dead was still nursing, and that especially was a very sad sight. The women as they were fleeing with their babes were killed together, shot right through, and the women who were very heavy with child were also killed. All the Native Americans fled in these three directions, and after most all of them had been killed a cry was made that all those who were not killed or wounded should come forth and they would be safe. Little boys who were not wounded came out of their places of refuge, and as soon as they came in sight a number of soldiers surrounded them and butchered them there."

Accounts of how the shooting started differ; regardless, the event signifies what historian and *Bury My Heart at Wounded Knee* author Dee Brown calls "the symbolic end of Indian freedom."

# THE FORT LARAMIE TREATY OF 1868

Signed in 1868, the last year that treaties were signed between the United States government and Indian tribes, this treaty provides a useful historical insight into the mutual understanding of reservations. The signatories to the treaty included the Arapaho people, as well as the following bands of Dakota (Sioux) people: Brule, Oglala, Minneconjou, Yanktonai, Hunkpapa, Blackfoot, Cuthead, Two Kettle, Sans Arc, and Santee.

ARTICLE 1.
From this day forward all war between the parties to this agreement shall forever cease. The Government of the United States desires peace, and its honor is hereby pledged to keep it. The Indians desire peace, and they now pledge their honor to maintain it.

*Below:* The sprawling Dakota (Sioux) encampment at Pine Ridge, South Dakota was photographed by G.E. Trager on November 28, 1890, shortly before the Wounded Knee massacre.

If bad men among the whites, or among other people subject to the authority of the United States, shall commit any wrong upon the person or property of the Indians, the United States will, upon proof made to the agent and forwarded to the Commissioner of Indian Affairs at Washington City, proceed at once to cause the offender to be arrested and punished according to the laws of the United States, and also reimburse the injured person for the loss sustained.

If bad men among the Indians shall commit a wrong or depredation upon the person or property of any one, white, black, or Indian, subject to the authority of the United States, and at peace therewith, the Indians herein named, agree that they will, upon proof made to their agent and notice by him, deliver up the wrong-doer to the United States, to be tried and punished according to its laws; and in case they willfully refuse so to do, the person injured shall be reimbursed for his loss from the annuities or other moneys due or to become due to them under this or other treaties made with the United States.

And the president, on advising with the Commissioner of Indian Affairs, shall prescribe such rules and regulations for ascertaining damages under the provisions of this article as in his judgment may be proper.

But no one sustaining loss while violating the provisions of this treaty or the laws of the United States shall be reimbursed therefore.

*Above:* Lone Wolf (Guipago), an important chief of the Kiowa, was photographed about 1868 by William Soule.

ARTICLE 2.

The United States agrees that the following district of country, to wit, viz: commencing on the east bank of the Missouri River where the 46th parallel of north latitude crosses the same, thence along low-water mark down said east bank to a point opposite where the northern line of the State of Nebraska strikes the river, thence west across said river, and along the northern line of Nebraska to the 104th degree of longitude west from Greenwich, thence north on said meridian to a point where the 46th parallel of north latitude intercepts the same, thence due east along said parallel to the place of beginning; and in addition thereto, all existing reservations on the east bank of said river shall be, and the same is, set apart for the absolute and undisturbed use and occupation of the Indians herein named, and for such other friendly tribes or individual Indians as

*Above:* An Oglala Dakota (Sioux) "burial" tree near Fort Laramie, Wyoming. Elevated interments were typical among the Plains tribes.

from time to time they may be willing, with the consent of the United States, to admit amongst them; and the United States now solemnly agrees that no persons except those herein designated and authorized so to do, and except such officers, agents, and employees of the government as may be authorized to enter upon Indian reservations in discharge of duties enjoined by law, shall ever be permitted to pass over, settle upon, or reside in the territory described in this article, or in such territory as may be added to this reservation for the use of said Indians, and henceforth they will and do hereby relinquish all claims or right in and to any portion of the United States or Territories, except such as is embraced within the limits aforesaid, and except as hereinafter provided.

ARTICLE 3.
If it should appear from actual survey or other satisfactory examination of said tract of land that it contains less than 160 acres of tillable land for each person who, at the time, may be authorized to reside on it under the provisions of this treaty, and a very considerable number of such persons shall be disposed to commence cultivating the soil as farmers, the United States agrees to set apart, for the use of said Indians, as herein provided, such additional quantity of arable land, adjoining to said reservation, or as

near to the same as it can be obtained, as may be required to provide the necessary amount.

## ARTICLE 4.

The United States agrees, at its own proper expense, to construct at some place on the Missouri River, near the center of said reservation, where timber and water may be convenient, the following buildings, to wit: a warehouse, a storeroom for the use of the agent in storing goods belonging to the Indians, to cost not less than $2,500; an agency-building for the residence of the agent, to cost not exceeding $3,000; a residence for the physician, to cost not more than $3,000; and five other buildings, for a carpenter, farmer, blacksmith, miller, and engineer, each to cost not exceeding $2,000; also a school- house or mission-building, so soon as a sufficient number of children can be induced by the agent to attend school, which shall not cost exceeding $5,000.

The United States agrees further to cause to be erected on said reservation, near the other buildings herein authorized, a good steam circular-saw mill, with a grist-mill and shingle-machine attached to the same, to cost not exceeding $8,000.

## ARTICLE 5.

The United States agrees that the agent for said Indians shall in the future make his home at the agency building; that he shall reside among them, and keep an office open at all times for the purpose of prompt and diligent inquiry into such matters of complaint by and against the Indians as may be presented for investigation under the provisions of their treaty stipulations, as also for the faithful discharge of other duties enjoined on him by law. In all cases of depredation on person or property he shall cause the evidence to be taken in writing and forwarded, together with his findings, to the Commissioner of Indian Affairs, whose decision, subject to the revision of the Secretary of the Interior, shall be binding on the parties to this treaty.

*Above:* Kiowa Chief Kicking Bird (Tene-angpote) was the grandson of a Crow captive. He was photographed by William Soule, circa 1868.

ARTICLE 6.

If any individual belonging to said tribes of Indians, or legally incorporated with them, being the head of a family, shall desire to commence farming, he shall have the privilege to select, in the presence and with the assistance of the agent then in charge, a tract of land within said reservation, not exceeding 320 acres in extent, which tract, when so selected, certified, and recorded in the "land-book," as herein directed, shall cease to be held in common, but the same may be occupied and held in the exclusive possession of the person selecting it, and of his family, so long as he or they may continue to cultivate it.

Any person over 18 years of age, not being the head of a family, may in like manner select and cause to be certified to him or her, for purposes of cultivation, a quantity of land not exceeding 80 acres in extent, and thereupon be entitled to the exclusive possession of the same as above directed.

For each tract of land so selected a certificate, containing a description thereof and the name of the person selecting it, with a certificate endorsed thereon that the same has been recorded, shall be delivered to the party entitled to it, by the agent, after the same shall have been recorded by him in a book to be kept in his office, subject to inspection, which said book shall be known as the "Sioux Land-Book."

The president may, at any time, order a survey of the reservation, and, when so surveyed, Congress shall provide for

*Below:* A group of Assiniboine men gathered for a dance at Poplar, Montana on the Fort Peck Reservation, circa 1882.

protecting the rights of said settlers in their improvements, and may fit the character of the title held by each.

The United States may pass such laws on the subject of alienation and descent of property between the Indians and their descendants as may be thought proper.

And it is further stipulated that any male Indians, over 18 years of age, of any band or tribe that is or shall hereafter become a party to this treaty, who now is or who shall hereafter become a resident or occupant of any reservation or Territory not included in the tract of country designated and described in this treaty for the permanent home of the Indians, which is not mineral land, nor reserved by the United States for special purposes other than Indian occupation, and who shall have made improvements thereon of the value of $200 or more, and continuously occupied the same as a homestead for the term of three years, shall be entitled to receive from the United States a patent for 160 acres of land including his said improvements, the same to be in the form of the legal subdivisions of the surveys of the public lands.

Upon application in writing, sustained by the proof of two disinterested witnesses, made to the register of the local land-office when the land sought to be entered is within a land district, and when the tract sought to be entered is not in any land district, then upon said application and proof being made to the Commissioner of the General Land Office, and the right of such Indian or Indians to enter such tract or tracts of land shall accrue and be perfect from the date of his first improvements thereon, and shall continue as long as he continues his residence and improvements, and no longer.

And any Indian or Indians receiving a patent for land under the foregoing provisions, shall thereby and from thenceforth become and be a citizen of the United States, and be

*Below:* Known as "Poison," this elderly Cheyenne woman was photographed in 1888 when she was roughly 100 years of age.

*Above:* The family of Stump Horn of the Southern Cheyenne was photographed with their horse-drawn travois by Christian Bartholomew in 1890.

entitled to all the privileges and immunities of such citizens, and shall, at the same time, retain all his rights to benefits accruing to Indians under this treaty.

## ARTICLE 7.

In order to insure the civilization of the Indians entering into this treaty, the necessity of education is admitted, especially of such of them as are or may be settled on said agricultural reservations, and they therefore pledge themselves to compel their children, male and female, between the ages of 6 and 16 years, to attend school.

It is hereby made the duty of the agent for said Indians to see that this stipulation is strictly complied with; and the United States agrees that for every 30 children between said ages who can be induced or compelled to attend school, a house shall be provided and a teacher competent to teach the elementary branches of an English education shall be furnished, who will reside among said Indians, and faithfully discharge his or her duties as a teacher. The provisions of this article to continue for not less than 20 years.

## ARTICLE 8.

When the head of a family or lodge shall have selected lands and received his certificate as above directed, and the agent shall be satisfied that he intends in good faith to commence cultivating the soil for a living, he shall be entitled to receive seeds and agricultural implements for the first year, not exceeding in value

$100, and for each succeeding year he shall continue to farm, for a period of three years more, he shall be entitled to receive seeds and implements as aforesaid, not exceeding in value $25.

And it is further stipulated that such persons as commence farming shall receive instruction from the farmer herein provided for, and whenever more than 100 persons shall enter upon the cultivation of the soil, a second blacksmith shall be provided, with such iron, steel, and other material as may be needed.

ARTICLE 9.

At any time after 10 years from the making of this treaty, the United States shall have the privilege of withdrawing the physician, farmer, blacksmith, carpenter, engineer, and miller herein provided for, but in case of such withdrawal, an additional sum thereafter of $10,000 per annum shall be devoted to the education of said Indians, and the Commissioner of Indian Affairs shall, upon careful inquiry into their condition, make such rules and regulations for the expenditure of said sum as will best promote the educational and moral improvement of said tribes.

ARTICLE 10.

In lieu of all sums of money or other annuities provided to be paid to the Indians herein named, under any treaty or treaties heretofore made, the United States agrees to deliver at the agency-house on the reservation herein named, on or before the first day of August of each year, for 30 years, the following articles, to wit:

For each male person over 14 years of age, a suit of good substantial woolen clothing, consisting of coat, pantaloons, flannel shirt, hat, and a pair of homemade socks.

For each female over 12 years of age, a flannel skirt, or the goods necessary to make it, a pair of woolen hose, 12 yards of calico, and 12 yards of cotton domestics.

For the boys and girls under the ages named, such flannel and cotton goods as may be needed to make each a suit as aforesaid, together with a pair of woolen hose for each. And in order that the Commissioner of Indian Affairs may be able to estimate

*Above:* Comanche warrior Asa Havi — also known as Bird Chief or Milky Way — was photographed in 1872 by Alexander Gardner.

*Above:* A group of Wichita children poses for posterity and the camera of Henry Peabody. Tepees were still in widespread use by Plains tribes in 1904, when the photograph was taken.

properly for the articles herein named, it shall be the duty of the agent each year to forward to him a full and exact census of the Indians, on which the estimate from year to year can be based.

And in addition to the clothing herein named, the sum of $10 for each person entitled to the beneficial effects of this treaty shall be annually appropriated for a period of 30 years, while such persons roam and hunt, and $20 for each person who engages in farming, to be used by the Secretary of the Interior in the purchase of such articles as from time to time the condition and necessities of the Indians may indicate to be proper. And if within the 30 years, at any time, it shall appear that the amount of money needed for clothing under this article can be appropriated to better uses for the Indians named herein, Congress may, by law, change the appropriation to other purposes; but in no event shall the amount of this appropriation be withdrawn or discontinued for the period named.

And the president shall annually detail an officer of the army to be present and attest the delivery of all the goods herein named to the Indians, and he shall inspect and report on the quantity and quality of the goods and the manner of their delivery.

And it is hereby expressly stipulated that each Indian over the age of four years, who shall have removed to and settled permanently upon said reservation and complied with the stipulations of this treaty, shall be entitled to receive from the

United States, for the period of four years after he shall have settled upon said reservation, one pound of meat and one pound of flour per day, provided the Indians cannot furnish their own subsistence at an earlier date. And it is further stipulated that the United States will furnish and deliver to each lodge of Indians or family of persons legally incorporated with them, who shall remove to the reservation herein described and commence farming, one good American cow, and one good well-broken pair of American oxen within 60 days after such lodge or family shall have so settled upon said reservation.

ARTICLE 11.
In consideration of the advantages and benefits conferred by this treaty, and the many pledges of friendship by the United States, the tribes who are parties to this agreement hereby stipulate that they will relinquish all right to occupy permanently the territory outside their reservation as herein defined, but yet reserve the right to hunt on any lands north of North Platte, and on the Republican Fork of the Smoky Hill River, so long as the buffalo may range thereon in such numbers as to justify the chase. And they, the said Indians, further expressly agree:

 1st. That they will withdraw all opposition to the construction of the railroads now being built on the plains.

 2nd. That they will permit the peaceful construction of any railroad not passing over their reservation as herein defined.

 3rd. That they will not attack any persons at home, or travelling, nor molest or disturb any wagon trains, coaches, mules, or cattle belonging to the people of the United States, or to persons friendly therewith.

 4th. They will never capture, or carry off from the settlements, white women or children.

 5th. They will never kill or scalp white men, nor attempt to do them harm.

 6th. They withdraw all pretense of opposition to the construction of the railroad now being built along the Platte River and westward to the Pacific Ocean, and they will not in future

*Above:* Little Raven — also known as Hosa or Young Crow — was an important chief of the Arapaho when he was photographed by William Soule in about 1868.

object to the construction of railroads, wagon-roads, mail-stations, or other works of utility or necessity, which may be ordered or permitted by the laws of the United States. But should such roads or other works be constructed on the lands of their reservation, the government will pay the tribe whatever amount of damage may be assessed by three disinterested commissioners to be appointed by the president for that purpose, one of said commissioners to be a chief or head-man of the tribe.

7th. They agree to withdraw all opposition to the military posts or roads now established south of the North Platte River, or that may be established, not in violation of treaties heretofore made or hereafter to be made with any of the Indian tribes.

### ARTICLE 12.
No treaty for the cession of any portion or part of the reservation herein described which may be held in common shall be of any validity or force as against the said Indians, unless executed and signed by at least 3/4 of all the adult male Indians, occupying or interested in the same; and no cession by the tribe shall be understood or construed in such manner as to deprive, without his consent, any individual member of the tribe of his rights to any tract of land selected by him, as provided in Article 6 of this treaty.

*Below:* A council between representatives of the Cheyenne and Arapaho tribes took place in 1900 at Seger Colony in Oklahoma.

ARTICLE 13.
The United States hereby agrees to furnish annually to the Indians the physician, teachers, carpenter, miller, engineer, farmer, and blacksmiths as herein contemplated, and that such appropriations shall be made from time to time, on the estimates of the Secretary of the Interior, as will be sufficient to employ such persons.

ARTICLE 14.
It is agreed that the sum of $500 annually, for three years from date, shall be expended in presents to the 10 persons of said tribe who in the judgment of the agent may grow the most valuable crops for the respective year.

ARTICLE 15.
The Indians herein named agree that when the agency-house or other buildings shall be constructed on the reservation named, they will regard said reservation their permanent home, and they will make no permanent settlement elsewhere; but they shall have the right, subject to the conditions and modifications of this treaty, to hunt, as stipulated in Article 11 hereof.

ARTICLE 16.
The United States hereby agrees and stipulates that the country north of the North Platte River and east of the summits of the Big Horn Mountains shall be held and considered to be unceded Indian territory, and also stipulates and agrees that no white person or persons shall be permitted to settle upon or occupy any portion of

*Below:* A Cheyenne woman and her dog travois, photographed near Lame Deer, Montana in 1922. Native Americans had used the dog travois for many centuries before the introduction of horses in the sixteenth century changed the lives of the Plains tribes forever.

*Above:* This photograph was taken in the studio of C.M. Bell in 1880 when a delegation of Dakota (Sioux) leaders made an inspection tour of the Carlisle Indian School in Pennsylvania. Seated are Red Dog, Little Wound, Red Cloud, American Horse and Red Shirt. The interpreter, John Bridgeman, stands in the rear.

the same; or without the consent of the Indians first had and obtained, to pass through the same; and it is further agreed by the United States that within 90 days after the conclusion of peace with all the bands of the Sioux Nation, the military posts now established in the territory in this article named shall be abandoned, and that the road leading to them and by them to the settlements in the Territory of Montana shall be closed.

ARTICLE 17.
It is hereby expressly understood and agreed by and between the respective parties to this treaty that the execution of this treaty and its ratification by the United States Senate shall have the effect, and shall be construed as abrogating and annulling all treaties and agreements heretofore entered into between the respective parties hereto, so far as such treaties and agreements obligate the United States to furnish and provide money, clothing, or other articles of property to such Indians and bands of Indians as become parties to this treaty, but no further.

In testimony of all which, we, the said commissioners, and we, the chiefs and head-men of the Brule band of the Sioux Nation, have hereunto set our hands and seals at Fort Laramie, Dakota Territory, this 29th day of April, in the year 1868.

# THE BLACKFEET RESERVATION, A CLOSE-UP VIEW

In examining the both the life and the history of the reservations and reserves in North America, there are many subtleties and nuances that demand the attention in detail that is perhaps not possible in a broad overview.

With this in mind, it is useful undertake a detailed case study. For this case study, we have chosen the Blackfeet Reservation of Montana because of its size, because its history is typical of the large Plains reservations established in the nineteenth century, and for the fact that it is located adjacent to the reserve of the related Blood people of Alberta.

The reservation is located just south of the Canadian border and to the west of Glacier National Park, in north central Montana. It was established in 1873, and, like many other reservations, it was established by presidential executive order in 1873. Another executive order in 1874 reduced reservation boundaries, while even more land was ceded to the government in subsequent agreements in 1888 and 1896.

And like many other reservations, the Blackfeet Reservation has been the scene of suffering and struggle, of the inevitable clash between white and Native American. Examining the circumstances that led to the reservation and how it survived during the ensuing years is one way of getting a better idea of how the reservation evolved, as well as how Native American life changed so drastically with their confinement to reservations and how they continued on despite such adversity.

Before the mid-1850s, the Blackfeet dominated an upper Great Plains expanse of land that encompassed the area north of the Missouri River and east of the Rocky Mountains. The Blackfeet people are actually comprised of four major (and closely related) tribes: the Siksika or Blackfeet proper, the Kainah or Blood, the Northern Pikuni or Northern Peigan, and the Southern Pikuni or Southern Peigan.

This conglomeration of Blackfeet — rivals at times but never enemies — shared many things, maintaining a common language, as well as similar customs and religious beliefs. Their lives focussed upon the buffalo, both as a source of food and economic wealth. Their contact with whites dated back well before a famous meeting between Meriwether Lewis and a small group of Peigan in 1806, but it wasn't until after 1830 that the Blackfeet became more involved with white settlers through commerce.

They became an integral link in the thriving buffalo hide trade. Unfortunately, their success in the trade was a mixed blessing: the Blackfeet were able to expand their territory and gain wealth, but the buffalo trade also fostered a greater involvement with the white economic system. The result was the further encroachment of white settlers upon Blackfeet lands.

Although the Blackfeet Reservation was officially established in 1851, 1855 marked the first United States

*Right:* Blackfeet Chief Curly Bear (Car-io-scuse), as photographed by DeLancey Gill in 1903.

government treaty with the Blackfeet. The treaty, which came to be known as Lame Bull's Treaty, was a direct response to pressures from the east to move further west. According to the terms of the treaty, the government was to give the Blackfeet $20,000 "in useful goods and services" annually, plus another $15,000 each year in order to promote their "civilization and Christianization" through various "white" institutions, such as instructional farms, schools and agricultural equipment.

In return the Blackfeet gave their word to remain at peace with the United States; they also promised to put an end to intertribal warfare in the region. Further-more, the Blackfeet agreed to remain on a circumscribed territory north of the Hell-gate-Musselshell River-Milk River line to the south and the east. United States citizens would be allowed to live in and travel through their lands. The construc-tion of roads, telegraph lines, military posts, missions and schools — as well as governmental agencies — would also be permitted. For the Blackfeet, life was quickly changing.

An agency was established in order to distribute the annual goods and services as specified by Lame Bull's Treaty. Located under the sheltering bluffs of the Upper Missouri River, Fort Benton became the central site of white activity in the area.

*Above:* A council taking place, circa 1920, in a large tepee on the Blackfeet Reservation in Montana.

At the time, the Blood, the Northern Blackfeet and some Peigan lived north of the United States-Canada border. Many, however, crossed the border to hunt, socialize and collect the treaty annu-ities. When it came time for distribution, the Indians discovered that most of the annuities consisted of items they already had because of their buffalo trade; either that or items such as coffee and rice (which the Blackfeet did not like) came under the rubric of so-called "useful goods." One important and lasting effect of the annuities was the beginning of a pattern of agency interven-tion and dependency. Once the buffalo were gone, the Blackfeet would have little choice left: they would have to depend on the government to survive.

Fort Benton continued to thrive, serving not only as a place for distribution and gathering, but also as a central connection of the Missouri lifeline to the Columbia River and the Pacific Northwest via the Mullan Road. The white population —

*Above:* A Blackfeet family with their horse-drawn travois, photographed on the Blackfeet Reservation, circa 1900.

whiskey traders, wolfers, prospectors, merchants and settlers—also increased, many of whom feared the Blackfeet. Hostilities and various skirmishes further manifested white fears. In response, the government erected another fort, Fort Shaw, by 1867.

Livestock and grazing also would play a significant part in this unfolding drama. Newly arrived white immigrants and established Montana stockmen placed larger numbers of herds onto the grassy plains. The buffalo were already decreasing in number, but the loss of grazing land certainly further contributed to their demise. The attractive Blackfeet lands were ripe for more open-range grazing, and, of course, more white settlers.

In 1873 and 1874 President Ulysses S. Grant signed two Executive Orders which reduced the reservation's southern boundary north of the Missouri and Marias rivers and Birch Creek. The Blackfeet were not consulted about the changes, and the federal government failed to offer payment for their gain. The orders did, however, lead to more and more guerrilla warfare, which had been going on sporadically since the 1860s in response to the overwhelming flood of white settlers and the loss of Blackfeet land.

Such tension between whites and Indians eventually culminated with an erroneous cavalry attack on a friendly Blackfeet camp in 1870. The Baker Massacre was disastrous: 173 Blackfeet dead and 140 women and children left to fend for themselves in

*Above:* White Buffalo (Wun-nes-tou) was a Blackfeet shaman interviewed and painted by George Catlin in the 1830s.

*Right:* This 1891 map shows the location of the Blackfeet Reservation, as well as other reservations in Montana. The size and shape of these have changed little since 1891.

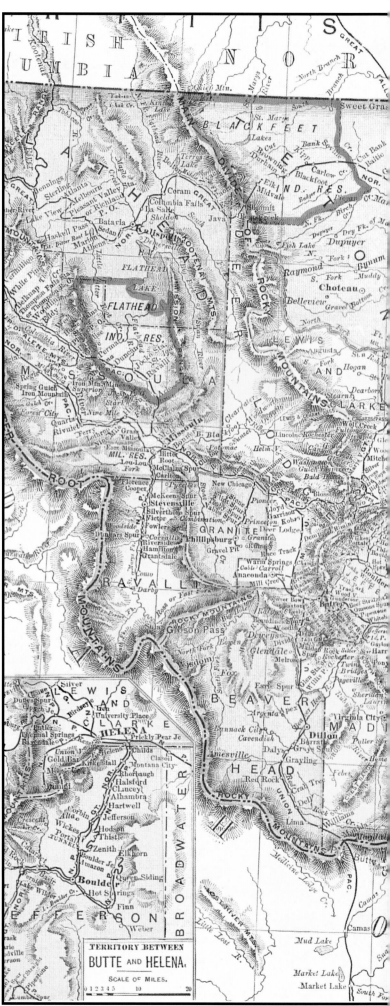

the cold Montana winter. Like the Wounded Knee Massacre that would occur 20 years later, the Baker Massacre seemed to signal the end of an era. The Black-feet tribes were beset with shock and indecision. They did not strike back. "Further war would only result in our extermination," said White Calf. The Native Americans were outnumbered, not only militarily but in terms of population numbers as well. Already the Black-feet population had dropped below 3,000, while the amount of white settlers inflated further.

As the 1870s came to a close, so did a way of life. The Blackfeet had witnessed the loss of huge amounts of territory. Their existence and their traditions had been threatened by the droves of whites settlers and the loss of the buffalo. Cattle also competed for range land with the buffalo. The Blackfeet still hunted buffalo, but the animal no longer provided the sustenance it once did.

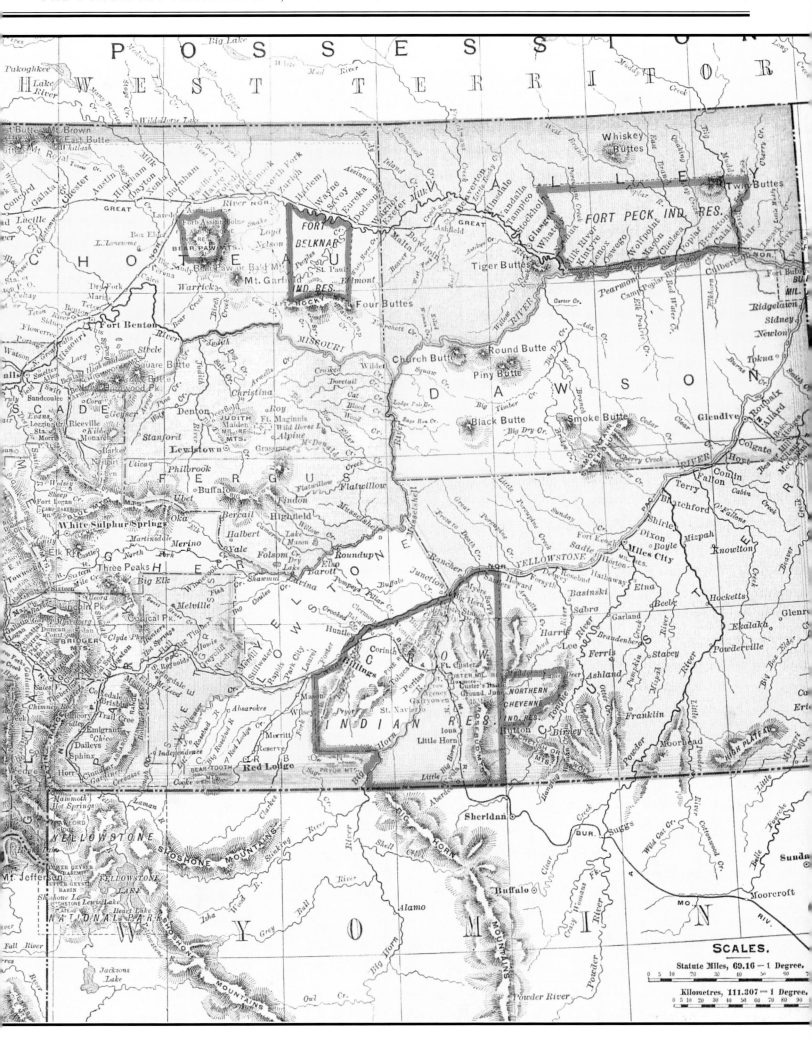

SCALES.

Statute Miles, 69.16 = 1 Degree.

Kilometres, 111.307 = 1 Degree.

So integral was the buffalo to the Blackfeet that Indian agent John W. Young reported that it would be all but impossible for them "to give up their nomadic life and settle down to farm or raise cattle." Dwindling buffalo herds eerily paralleled the reduction in the Blackfeet: the 1880 federal census cited approximately 2,200 Blackfeet, as opposed to a white population of more than 12,000 persons (consisting of the counties of Chouteau, Lewis and Clark, and Meagher).

The Blackfeet managed to adjust to their reduced reservation lands. But soon the land itself became useless. It was barren. Grass and water had dried up. Finally the buffalo were gone too and bands of Blackfeet roamed the area, still holding on to the past. The buffalo hunters now faced the inevitable and began their trek west to their last hope: the government rations of Old Agency, located on lower Badger Creek.

*Above:* A group of Blackfeet elders pose before a tepee on the Blackfeet Reservation.

Unfortunately for the hungry and weary Blackfeet, the rations owed them by treaty arrangement were not delivered. Cases of smallpox also contributed to the misery. During the Starvation Winter of 1883-1884, approximately 600 Indians died. The Blackfeet would have to resign themselves to the coming of reservation life, something perhaps unimaginable only 30 years before when Lame Bull's Treaty was signed. According to Blackfeet historian William E. Farr, "As they became reservation Indians their loss only grew, and yet it was so difficult to assess by European immigrant standards. It was more than a loss of a way of life, but was, confusing as it may sound, a loss of home in their own homeland. Now nothing could be taken for granted. There were at once too many choices and yet no choice. The Blackfeet had begun their reservation stay."

In the years following the Starvation Winter, Blackfeet numbers dropped to a mere 2,000. The drive to again reduce reservation land intensified. White settlers wrote their congressmen, asking for more grazing areas to be granted to them, while newspapers featured editorials calling for the acquisition of more land. *The Helena Herald* wrote that "These ranges are needed for our cattle and they are of no use in the world to the Indian."

The coming of James Hill's Great Northern Railway provided yet another opportunity for white Montanans to call for the reduction of Indian lands.

The result was a "land sale." In late 1886 a new Treaty Commission was appointed to negotiate with the Blackfeet, the Sioux,

*Above:* A photographer setting up to photograph a Blackfeet encampment on the reservation, near the high mountains of Glacier National Park.

the Assiniboine, and the Gros Ventre. Blackfeet elders White Calf and Three Sons met with the Treaty Commission and, in early February 1887, signed away most of their land. The reservation boundaries were again altered. A significant eastern section of the earlier reservation was dissolved; the Blackfeet would now be limited to a small, rectangular area located just under the Rockies. The Blackfeet were to be compensated with $150,000 annually for a total of ten years, the money to go toward the purchase of livestock and equipment, to build schools and homes, and to foster economic independence and cultural assimilation.

However, assimilation and the "civilizing" of the Blackfeet failed to happen overnight. In addition, a revolving door of government agents (seven during the 1886-1900 period) made it even more difficult for the Blackfeet to better their condition. While the Blackfeet's situation worsened and they tried to acclimate themselves to reservation life, whites in the area thrived; prospectors blasted and dug on reservation land (which was illegal); cattle continued to trespass on the reservation, eating valuable grass land; and the Great Northern Railway made its first trek across reservation land in the early 1890s.

Because of these and other factors the Blackfeet spread out. No longer was Old Agency on Badger Creek a centralized place. In 1895, another land purchase transpired between the Blackfeet and the United States government. For $1.5 million over another ten-year period, a mountainous portion of the western reservation was sold — "ceded land" that would become part of Glacier

National Park. Although reluctant to part with the land, the move was pragmatic more than anything else. It was hoped that the money generated would help the Blackfeet survive — and perhaps thrive — in twentieth century America, as more and more people had settled down to a stationary existence, some gaining experience as stockmen, some learning to farm.

With the turn of the century, the Blackfeet found their reservation under the direct control of governmental management; specifically, the Blackfeet Reservation, like all reservations, was governed by the Indian Service in Washington, DC. The superior authority on any reservation was the Indian agent, sometimes called "major," and later a "superintendent." The agent was bestowed with so much power and authority that he was also often referred to as a czar.

In Washington, the government's Indian policy failed to take into account the specific land or culture of an Indian tribe. A reservation was, simply, a reservation: they were all, in essence, the same. The model for a reservation during the early years of the twentieth century consisted of the following uniform ingredients: agency plant, tribal police, boarding schools, missions and licensed traders. Perhaps most important was the use of education, which became a tool to further "civilize" and assimilate the Native Americans. Two major boarding schools were erected on the Blackfeet Reservation in 1907. Among other things, the schools taught methods of farming. It was all part of the government's ongoing effort to turn warriors into farmers,

*Above and Below right:* These rare, 1930s color photographs show a Blackfeet "pow-wow," or festival, at Browning, Montana on the reservation.

*Above right:* A group of Blackfeet greet tourists near the Glacier Park Lodge in East Glacier, Montana, circa 1940. The Lodge is actually located on the Blackfeet Reservation, about a mile from Glacier National Park.

nomadic hunters into stationary people, Native Americans into whites.

Although many Blackfeet adopted a certain amount of the white man's ways, they still sought to retain a sense of their past and their collective heritage. One such enduring tradition was the Sun Dance. The purpose of the event was to gather the various Blackfeet bands living on the reservation during the early days of summer. Once assembled, they would gather in a great circle camp. A medicine lodge or "okan" was constructed in the middle of the circle, and thus served as a holy place of prayer, sacrifice and spiritual renewal.

As whites desired the eradication of such "heathen" activities, the Blackfeet moved the celebration so that it would coincide with the Fourth of July celebration. The change occurred around 1900. However, white efforts to end the Sun Dance did not cease. In 1910, a Catholic missionary who had been working with the Blackfeet for 40 years penned an article entitled "The Fourth of July Dishonored." In the article Father J.B. Carroll writes that the Blackfeet celebrate the Sun Dance on the Fourth of July "not because of our free institutions and national greatness, but because it reminds them of the darkest days of heathenism and bloodshed, because it is the day on which they parade as real savages in their war paints and war dances." Despite such opposition, the Sun Dance continues to this day, providing a source of renewal and hope for the Blackfeet people.

While bureaucratic debate meandered on in Washington, the Blackfeet unfortunately deteriorated after 1900. They tried their hand at cattle ranching and farming, but progress was slow and government support inconsistent. Debate on how the reservation should be managed went back and forth between the years 1905 and 1921. Meanwhile, attracted by the Homestead Acts of 1909 and 1912, white settlers poured into Montana. Close to 90,000 homesteaders filed the appropriate papers at land offices in Great Falls and Miles City between 1905 and 1919.

In contrast, the Blackfeet were faced with a severe drought period lasting from 1917 to 1920, which led to widespread poverty, sickness, hunger and malnutrition. The Blackfeet population hovered around 3,000, with two-thirds of that amount receiving government rations.

A new agent, Fred C. Campbell, arrived in 1920 and declared the Blackfeet's involvement in the cattle industry a terrible failure. Instead, Campbell advocated a policy of farming and irrigation. That policy again changed in 1929 with the arrival

*Above:* Noted author Mary Roberts Rinehart during a visit to the Blackfeet Reservation.

*Above:* A Blackfeet gathering in the St. Mary
Valley of Montana, near Glacier National Park.

of Campbell's successor, Forrest Stone, who thought economic
development and self-sufficiency for the Blackfeet would be best
achieved through sheep and wool. The plan, however, was
hindered by the coming of the Great Depression. The years
preceding World War II also saw little change on the reservation.
Feuds between full bloods and mixed bloods continued to esca-
late. Employment was scarce and the government failed to
provide any kind of consistent policy. Economic independence
for the Blackfeet was far from being realized. "Despite the expen-
diture of millions of dollars of Blackfeet money and fifty years of
Indian Service activity, little had changed since 1886," writes
Farr. "The reservation and its institutions had failed. When the
1940s began, the Blackfeet were as dependent a people as they
had been following the end of the buffalo."

The postwar era did witness some notable changes: Blackfeet
who had enlisted or worked in nearby shipyards did not return to
the reservation; the older generation gave way to the new; the
modernization of the reservation and the intrusion of the white
world continued; and the reservation was now a permanent
institution, a way of life for the Blackfeet people, who were now
— unlike their ancestor — reservation Indians.

Yet despite the enormous changes over the past century and
a half, traditions still carry on. Isolated and frustrated, dealing
with issues and uncertainties that have never seemed to get
resolved, the Blackfeet manage to maintain their culture, and to
retain a sense of pride in their heritage. The struggle has paid off.

In contrast to the low population numbers during the early
part of the twentieth century, there are now approximately 9,000
enrolled Blackfeet tribal members — 7,000 of whom live on or
near the reservation.

*Left:* The heart of Browning, Montana, the largest city on the Blackfeet Reservation and the seat of tribal government.

*Above:* The Museum of the Plains Indian at Browning is managed by the Bureau of Indian Affairs and offers exhibits of Plains Indian history, art and ethnography.

*Above left:* Entering Browning, Montana from the south. The city is also home to the Blackfeet Community College, a tribally chartered institution fully accredited as a two-year college. In cooperation with the University of Great Falls and Montana State University in Bozeman, the community college offers undergraduate, graduate and doctorate courses.

# ALLOTMENT AND BEYOND

In the years following the Civil War, much of the attention in the United States remained focused on healing the war wounds and on Reconstruction. In terms of the government's Native American policy, one significant alteration had occurred: armed resistance against the government was practically over. Thus, the government's effort to assimilate the entire native population became much more efficient.

Between 1873 and 1877, under the presidency of Ulysses S. Grant, the United States government's official policy toward the Indians was called "the Peace Policy."

One of the main tenets of the Peace Policy was the reservation. Although it would be short-lived, the goals of the policy were familiar: acculturation, "civilizing" the Indian and perpetuating white control over the Native American.

According to the Secretary of the Interior's summary of the plan in 1873: "The so-called Peace Policy sought, first, to place the Native Americans upon reservations as rapidly as possible, where they could be provided for in such manner as the dictates of humanity and Christian civilization require. Being thus placed upon reservations, they will be removed from such contiguity to our frontier settlements as otherwise will lead, necessarily, to frequent outrages, wrongs and disturbances of the public peace. On these reservations they can be taught, as fast as possible, the arts of agriculture, and such pursuits as are incident to civilization. . . . Their intellectual, moral, and religious culture can be prosecuted, and thus it is hoped that humanity and kindness may take the place of barbarity and cruelty."

Military control was less of an issue on the reservations, but the army still combed the Plains area, corralling Indians and coercing them to live on the reservations assigned to them.

Uncooperative Indians caught outside the confines of the reservation were presumed to be at war. Such outlaws were therefore liable to military reprisal. It was this definition that had led to Custer's disastrous attack at the Little Big Horn in 1876. By being off the reservation, Sitting Bull's people were technically declaring war on the United States.

Meanwhile, those Indians living on reservations were subject to the authority of a Bureau of Indian Affairs agent who was appointed by either a missionary society or a church board. Part of Grant's policy included bringing religious leaders into the governing of the Native Americans in order to root out corruption, as well as to bring the word of God to the Indians. The reservation itself was thought to be a means of taming the "wild" Indian, as a way to "prosecute" and eradicate a previous way of life.

In addition to the effort to restrict Indians to reservations, the government also desired to detribalize Indians. This transformation had already been in effect since 1871, when the policy of treaty making was ended.

*Right:* Sharp Nose (Ta-qua-wi), an Arapaho chief, was photographed in 1884 wearing US Army captain's bars.

No longer were Native American tribes sovereign nations; they were expected to discard their communal ways and adopt the economic and intellectual atmosphere of individualism, as advanced by capitalism and the transcendentalist thought of writers such as Emerson, Thoreau and Whitman.

To further implement the assimilation of the Native American, Indian education was centralized in the 1880s. A bureaucracy was established within the Bureau of Indian Affairs to oversee the plan. Over the next decade, the federal government would continue to tighten its supervision over Indian education.

Passage of the Dawes General Allotment Act in 1887 was, in part, a reaction to the Indians' refusal to embrace the ways of the white man. The government felt it needed to take extreme action in order to forcibly assimilate the Indians. The intent of the act was to break up tribal land holdings, allot small parcels of 40 to 100 acres to Native American families or individuals and eventually convert Native Americans into "civilized" farmers, and thus earn a place within the larger white community. Additionally, the "surplus lands" on the reservations were opened up to settlement.

Congressman Henry Dawes, author of the act and "a friend of the Indian," once expressed his faith in the civilizing power of private property with the claim that to be civilized was to "wear civilized clothes, cultivate the ground, live in houses, ride in Studebaker wagons, send children to school, drink whiskey [and] own property."

Ignoring Indian protests against allotment and the fact that the practice of private property was contrary to the Native American tradition of communal property rights, the Dawes Act become the cornerstone of the government's Indian policy during the latter half of the nineteenth century and the early decades of the twentieth century. The policy, however, failed miserably and amounted to a major disaster for the tribes. In the nearly 50 years of the allotment period, Native American land holdings were reduced from more than 136 million acres in 1887 to less than 50 million acres in 1934, when the policy was abandoned completely with passage of the Indian Reorganization Act.

*Above:* Eagle Ribs (Pe-toh-pee-kiss) was a prominent Blackfeet warrior boasting eight scalps when he was sketched by George Catlin in the 1830s.

*Right:* Woman-Who-Strikes-Many (Ah-kay-ee-pix-en) and the shaman Iron Horn (In-ne-o-cose) were among the Blackfeet who met George Catlin on his journey into the upper Missouri country in the 1830s.

Another landmark decision came in 1919, when the power to set up executive order reservations was ended by Congress. Today, a reservation can be created (or expanded) by a specific act of Congress or by the Secretary of the Interior, acting under the authority of the Indian Reorganization Act.

The period between 1921 and 1945 saw a reevaluation of the United States government's Indian policy. The Wheeler-Howard Act (a.k.a. the Indian Citizenship Act) of 1924 granted citizenship to all Indians, although initially this did little to improve their status. Under the provisions of the act, a $10 million revolving fund was established to make loans to Indian tribes.

However, in 1928, a scathing report by the Brookings Institution in Washington, DC brought much needed attention to the plight of reservation life. The report contained strong criticism of the whole acculturation policy of allotment and recommended far-reaching changes. It also led to the drafting of the Indian Reorganization Act of 1934 ("a Magna Carta for the red men," said one historian), which aimed to grant Native Americans greater autonomy in managing their affairs. Tribes were now permitted to organize their own institutions. Individual rights were also expanded. Besides halting allotment, the act additionally prohibited the sale of Native American lands to non-Indians.

Despite these apparent gains, the Bureau of Indian Affairs retained veto power over most tribal decisions, including those concerning financial matters. The intent of the Indian Reorganization Act may have been to grant Indians greater autonomy and self-sufficiency, but the reality of it proved to be quite different. Bureau of Indian Affairs officials failed to push for implementation of policies and programs that would eventually assist tribes and reservations in forming self-sustaining communities.

As North America entered the Great Depression and later World War II, Washington-appointed officials still controlled governance of the reservations. Because of the poor economic situation and the subsequent war effort, governmental support and assistance for the reservations was drastically reduced.

The Indian was hardly a priority. However, after the war the United States government began another phase in its Indian policy and implemented yet another change in direction by seeking to terminate all federal responsibility toward the Indians. The policy was a direct reversal of the long history of dependency that had been forced upon reservation Indians — those whose tribal resources had depleted over the years, mostly by ceding their lands to the government in exchange for promised assistance.

It was also during the postwar era that a system of area offices was established and area directors were made responsible for administering all bureau programs within their geographical locations. The Bureau of Indian Affairs currently functions through a three-tier organizational structure topped by the central, or headquarters, office in Washington, DC.

At the second, or mid-management, level are the 12 area offices located throughout the United States, which have various authorities over geographical regions. The final organizational components are the agencies, which provide services to one or more tribes. Lines of authority within the Department of Interior run from the cabinet-level Interior Secretary to the sub-cabinet level Assistant Secretary for Indian Affairs, which is the top Indian affairs post in the federal government. The Assistant Secretary is appointed by the president and confirmed by the United States Senate.

The government-to-government aspect of federal /tribal relations has received some serious assaults through the years. In particular, the allotment period had a severe effect on the ability of tribal governments to function, and the termination era in the 1950s threatened the entire structure of the relationship. In recent years, however, tribes have adopted measures to strengthen their tribal governments and take control of their own affairs. The Bureau of Indian Affairs is supportive of this process.

For example, in 1985, 440 self-determination grants went to tribes to strengthen their tribal governments. Also, tribal government services of the bureau are being expanded to improve and strengthen the technical support provided to tribal

*Below:* A delegation of men from the Zuni Reservation, as photographed by John Hillers in 1879.

*Above:* A delegation from the Otoe Reservation, wearing claw necklaces and fur turbans, as photographed by John Hillers in 1881.

governments and tribal court systems. Special initiatives will be directed to formal training, specialized guidance, improvement of tribal governing document codes, and other regulatory controls that will enhance a tribe's capacity to govern.

Meanwhile, the government's termination policy was further buoyed by a 1953 congressional resolution calling for termination of federal supervision of reservations in five states and seven additional locations. In addition to the resolution, ten termination bills were introduced in the next session of Congress. Six of the ten managed to pass. In summary, the laws ended all special federal services, providing for the termination of federal trusteeship over tribal and individuals' lands, resources, and funds, and the withdrawal of all other wardship and federal obligations signifying a special status for Native Americans.

Termination was to occur as soon as possible. Tribal members would then be subject to the same state laws and jurisdiction as other citizens. Again ignoring Native American protest over so radical and abrupt a change, the Bureau of Indian Affairs' responsibility for several tribes was dissolved. Among those affected (10,000 Indians in all) were the Klamath of Oregon, the tribes of western Oregon, the Menominee tribe of Wisconsin and six tribes in Utah. The main proponent of the policy was Senator Arthur Watkins of Utah, who declared: "Following in the footsteps of the Emancipation Proclamation . . . I see the following words emblazoned in letters of fire above the heads of Indians —

"These people shall be free!"

*Above:* For reasons that are lost to history, Lone Bear (Tar-lo) of the Kiowa dressed as an Osage boy and painted stripes on his forehead when he was photographed by William Soule in about 1874.

*Left:* This Papago basket-maker was photographed in Arizona in 1916 by H.T. Cory.

*Right:* Pacer (Essa-queta) was a Kiowa-Apache chief photographed by William Soule in about 1874.

Needless to say, the effect of termination on reservation life was not emancipation, but disaster. Although the policy continued until at least 1958, supporters of the policy of termination dwindled. In 1970, the Nixon administration repudiated the termination policy, calling for self-determination for Native Americans without termination of federal services or trusteeship.

A presidential message on July 8, 1970 announced the formation of a new policy: before federal support is to be removed from a reservation, there must be an adequate guarantee that the residents will be given the opportunity and support to form their own government and to control their own institutions. The means for self-support must be made available before the government withdraws all assistance.

In theory, tribal governments are autonomous institutions, able to assume control over their affairs unless prohibited by Congress. In reality, however, the federal government maintains ultimate rule, reserving the right to veto all tribal laws, codes, ordinances, and financial arrangements. Indians are thus denied control over their educational, social and welfare institutions, as well as their own resources. It is not surprising then that during the early 1970s some tribes — including the Pima Maricopa in Arizona and the Zuni Pueblos in New Mexico — sought to take over Bureau of Indian Affairs functions.

The political activism of the 1960s and early 1970s was also widespread among the general Indian population. The surge in activism among native peoples led some to label the movement as "Red Power," drawing the analogy from the black movement at the time. Besides the politicization of reservation Indians, many urban Indians also formed political organizations during the 1960s, the most famous being the American Indian Movement (AIM). The occupation of Alcatraz and the takeover of the Bureau of Indian Affairs building in Washington are just two examples of Native American activism and the desire to

*Above:* Young Kaivavit and her father, a Paiute arrow-maker, posed nervously for Clement Powell in front of their northern Arizona home on October 4, 1872.

*Above:* A group of young Paiute horsemen on the Kaibab Plateau of northern Arizona, circa 1871.

campaign for Indian rights, to draw attention to the plight of the Indians (both their past and present) and to alter the harsh conditions that continued to prevail on reservations.

The issue of termination, however, remained (and still remains) a vexing question for the Indians and for the reservation — as well as for those governmental officials involved in crafting contemporary Indian policy. Should Native Americans sever their relationship with the United States? The answer is complex, one that involves a number of factors, including history and culture, and the promise of a better future, but also the possibility of an uncertain one and a tenuous, yet dependent, relationship between the Indians and the United States government. The debate continues unresolved to this day.

*Right:* A woman drying peaches at the Isleta Pueblo in New Mexico, circa 1900.

*Below:* A group of Apache men playing the hoop and pole game, circa 1900.

*Left:* This Uainuint Paiute warrior posed with his old single-action rifle for John Hillers in 1873.

*Below:* This girl wearing beads was photographed on Arizona's Havasupai Reservation in 1900 by Henry Peabody.

# Exploring the Trust Relationship

According to the United States Bureau of Indian Affairs, the trust relationship between the United States and Indian tribes and Alaska Natives "cannot be precisely defined to satisfy all it entails." For this reason, as the bureau concedes, "misunderstandings sometimes arise, and often parties will disagree on the extent of the trust." The trust agreement is not spelled out. There is no trust agreement, with all its ramifications, that may be found in any single document. Rather, the trust is an evolving doctrine that has been expanded over the years to meet changing situations and changing times.

As the Bureau of Indian Affairs points out, because the trust relationship is not specifically defined, this does not mean that it is lacking in importance or significance. The trust is an established legal and moral obligation requiring the United States to protect and enhance the property and resources of Indian tribes.

The trust responsibility was first enunciated by the courts in Cherokee Nation v. Georgia, which was handed down in 1831. The significance of the high court opinion, written by Chief Justice John Marshall, is found in a discussion of the legal status of Indian tribes and their relationship with the federal government.

Marshall characterized this relationship as "perhaps unlike that of any other two people in existence," and said it was "marked by peculiar and cardinal distinctions that exist nowhere else." He then invoked the trust relationship between Indian tribes and the United States by saying it "resembles that of a ward to his guardian."

The use of such words as "guardian" and "ward" may have seemed appropriate in the nineteenth century, but today the relationship more properly should be described as involving a "trustee" and "beneficiary."

In common law, a guardian is under the supervision of a court and is not required to consult with the ward in carrying out his duties. This is distinguished from the trust relationship, which is sometimes viewed as a partnership agreement. For example, the consent of Indian tribes is required in order to dispose of property. Also, there is a much broader accountability required by the trustee to the beneficiary than would be found in a guardianship.

This obligation has often been referred to as "fiduciary," meaning founded on trust or confidence. Through the years, courts have agreed with Marshall that our law has no direct parallel to this trust relationship, and it has been described as being "unique," or "solemn," or "special," or "moral."

The trust responsibility of the United States with regard to the land and other natural resources of Indian tribes and Alaska Natives is a direct outgrowth of English law and practice, which held that title to newly-discovered lands was in the Crown, or government, but subject to a compensable right of occupancy by the aboriginal people.

*Right:* A young woman named Miss Waters, possibly of the Nez Perce tribe, sits astride her pinto, holding a bow.

Title to land is held in trust for tribes by the United States. In certain instances, land is held in trust by the United States for individual Indians. Some tribal funds also are held in trust and, in some cases, funds are held in trust for individual Native Americans.

In regard to land, the trust responsibility is extensive, encompassing not only the land itself but anything to do with the land. Thus, the minerals under it, the water flowing over it, and the grass that grows upon it all are elements of the trust estate. As the operating arm of the Secretary of Interior, the Bureau of Indian Affairs has a responsibility to carry out the management and protection of these resources.

Although Cherokee Nation v. Georgia involved a treaty, court decisions have held that the trust relationship may be created by other means, such as statutes, agreements and executive orders. The trust consists of a series of laws passed by Congress, regulations promulgated pursuant to these laws, and federal administrative practice. There is a separate body of Indian trust law developed by the federal courts based on federal court decisions.

*Above:* A Pomo woman pounding acorns with a stone pestle in a basket mortar at Ukiah, California, circa 1890.

*Right:* Lance (Meraparapa) of the Mandan, circa 1894.

*Below:* A Potawatomi Farm, circa 1877.

# RESERVATIONS OF THE SOUTHWEST

Today, the majority of United States reservations are found in the western part of the country, and the largest of these is the Navajo Reservation. Covering more than 24,000 square miles in northeastern Arizona, northwestern New Mexico and southeastern Utah, it is larger than all of New England excluding Maine. Neighboring towns include Flagstaff, Winslow and Holbrook, Arizona, as well as Gallup, New Mexico.

The Navajo people also constitute the largest American Indian tribe in the United States, numbering more than 200,000 people. The Navajo speak a language belonging to the Athapaskan linguistic family. Their name is derived from a Keresan Indian word; they originally called themselves Dinneh, or "the people."

Unlike reservations on the northern Plains and elsewhere, the Navajo Reservation, and the Hopi Reservation — which it entirely surrounds — are examples of reservations that were created for Native Americans already living in a given area.

Located in northeastern Arizona and occupying parts of Navajo and Coconino counties, the Hopi Reservation encompasses approximately 1,542,306 acres, of which 911,000 acres are identified as the Hopi Partitioned Lands. The reservation consists of three major mesas rising up to 7,200 feet, and is surrounded by low altitude deserts and gullies. One of the reservation's most striking sights is Oraibi, which is believed by some to be the oldest continuously inhabited settlement in the United States, perhaps dating to as early as 1150 AD.

In southeastern Arizona, the San Carlos Apache Indian Reservation spans Gila, Graham and Pinal counties. It was first established as a reservation by President Grant's Executive Order on November 9, 1871. Apaches are descendants of the Athapaskan family, who migrated to the Southwest in the tenth century. Many bands of Apache, as well as Mohave and Yuma Indians, were relocated from their traditional homelands, which extended through wide areas of Arizona and New Mexico, to the site of the current reservation. Later, separate reservations were created for the Mohave and Yuma tribes. United States 70, a main, scenic route between Phoenix and Lordsburg, New Mexico, runs through the 2,854 square mile reservation that ranges from low plains and rolling desert hills to pine-forested, high-mountain country.

Both the Navajo and their linguistic relatives, the Apache, are relative newcomers to the Southwest. They are thought to have arrived in the region not more than 500 years ago, moving south from the homeland of other Athapaskan speakers in northwest Canada and interior Alaska.

They were preceded by the Anasazi people, whose name means "the ancient ones." The Anasazi settled in the Southwest in the first century, and by the eleventh century they were building elaborate, multi-storied cities at such placed as Mesa Verde in Colorado and at

*Right:* Pahlowahtiwa, the governor of the Zuni Reservation, circa 1880.

Canyon de Chelly in Arizona. For reasons that are not completely understood, the Anasazi culture had collapsed by the fourteenth century. Soon after, the region was inherited by the Navajo newcomers.

Once in the Southwest, the Navajo underwent a series of culture changes in adapting to a natural environment vastly different from that of the north and as a result of new contacts with long-established southwestern peoples, particularly the Pueblo Indians.

Originally nomadic, the Navajo subsisted through hunting and the gathering of wild plant foods. After learning techniques of dry farming (without irrigation) from the Pueblo peoples, they began to raise maize, beans, squash and melons. Livestock, particularly sheep, acquired from the Spanish during the early seventeenth century, also became important in their economy.

*Below:* A man working with a hoe in a cornfield on the Hopi Reservation, circa 1910.

The Navajo persistently raided the villages of the Pueblo Indians, as well as those of the Spanish and, later, the Mexican colonists from the 1600s on. After the Anglo-Americans took possession of the Southwest, the raids continued until 1863, when most of the Navajo were rounded up by militiamen under Kit Carson. They were then sent to a detention facility at Fort Sumner in New Mexico for a total of four years. In 1868, a treaty was concluded with the Navajo, in which they agreed to settle on a reservation in their former homeland. At the time they numbered about 9,000.

In 1923, the Navajo Tribal Council was founded in order for tribe members to deal collectively with the United States. Traditionally, the Navajo had no centralized tribal government. In the past, autonomous bands had existed; each occupied a definite territory and had dual leaders, one for war and one for peace. Only rarely did two or more bands cooperate in any activity, even warfare.

Today, the Navajo are considered to possess one of the best-preserved native American cultures in North America. Their social structure is based on bonds of kinship, with descent traced through the mother. The preferred pattern is the extended family, consisting of at least two adult generations: an older woman and

*Above:* With several Hopi people observing patiently, Dancer's Rock on the Hopi Reservation at Walpi, Arizona, was photographed in 1879 by John Hillers.

her husband and unmarried children, plus her married daughters and their husbands and children. The members of an extended family usually live near each other and cooperate in such activities as house building, farming and herding. The traditional Navajo dwelling is the hogan, a structure usually with six or eight sides, constructed of logs and covered with earth.

The most important Navajo craft is the weaving of fine rugs, learned from the Pueblo people in the late seventeenth century, and traditionally performed on upright looms by women. Also important is silversmithing, which was learned in the nineteenth century from Mexican smiths; typical craft objects include beautifully worked silver, as well as turquoise jewelry, which was often decorated with squash blossom symbols.

Central to the traditional Navajo world view of the universe is the belief that the world contains hostile as well as friendly forces. If the universal harmony is disturbed, illness, death, or other disasters may result. The Navajo believe that all illness, physical or mental, has supernatural causes, which can be ascertained only by a rite of divination. To affect a cure, the doctor-priest or singer (hatali) prescribes one of many Navajo chants; in addition, the patient is often placed during the curing ceremony on an elaborate and beautifully colored sand painting, which depicts events in the life of the supernatural. Certain Navajo ceremonies involve the ritual consumption of peyote.

Despite managing to continue their culture and traditions, the Navajos—like many other Indians—presently face persistent economic problems in their arid homeland.

The Navajo population continues to increase rapidly, despite rates of infant and child mortality that remain disproportionately high compared with national figures. Their subsistence economy continues to be based on agriculture, with almost every reservation family raising at least part of its food. In recent years, sheep raising has been reduced because of the serious deterioration of the Navajo grasslands through overgrazing and erosion. Arts and crafts, especially weaving and silversmithing, are minor sources of income, but the Navajo have become increasingly reliant on wage employment. The discovery of natural gas, uranium, and other minerals has helped to provide new sources of tribal income, but the Navajo are still among the poorest Native American groups in the United States.

Another important native group in the American Southwest are the Pueblo — the word literally means "people" in Spanish — of New Mexico's Rio Grande Valley. Interestingly, they had, by the fifteenth century, established cities with multi-story permanent dwellings. Unlike the Anasazi, who built such structures in earlier times, the Pueblo tribes have continued to live in their cities to this day.

The pueblos, as the cities themselves are called, became the subject of Spanish interest — and Spanish colonial folklore — in the sixteenth century. In 1539, Father Marcos de Niza made a journey into the Rio Grande Valley, and returned to Mexico City with tales of "seven cities of gold."

This naturally interested the Spanish colonials. In 1540, the Spanish explorer Francisco Vasquez de Coronado set out to explore the region north of Mexico and to find the golden cities. With Father de Niza as part of his expedition, Coronado sailed as far north as possible in the Sea of Cortez and made landfall near the mouth of the Colorado River. From here, he set out overland

*Above:* A Navajo woman weaving a blanket on a loom, somewhere on the Navajo Reservation, circa 1910.

*Above:* The Speaker Chief section of the ancient Anasazi cliff dwelling at Mesa Verde, Colorado.

*Right:* The Square Tower at Mesa Verde. The area that is now Mesa Verde National Park has been under the protection of the US National Park Service since 1906, the first such area set aside to preserve the works of human beings. The Anasazi people who built these structures, lived here for 700 years until about 1200. Their basic construction material was sandstone, which they shaped into rectangular blocks about the size of a loaf of bread. The mortar between the blocks was a mix of mud and water. Rooms averaged about 48 square feet, space enough for two or three persons. By 1000 the Anasazi had advanced from pole-and-adobe construction to skillful stone masonry. Their walls of thick double-coursed stone often rose two or three stories high and were joined together into units of 50 rooms or more.

*Left:* Herding sheep and goats on the Navajo Reservation today recalls the practices of the past.

*Below:* Navajo men shearing sheep, circa 1940. Sheep are an important part of the traditional economic base on the Navajo Reservation.

*Right:* In 1936, H. Armstrong Roberts photographed this young lamb investigating a Navajo baby on a cradleboard.

*Below:* A pair of modern Navajo children wearing traditional turquoise jewelry and costumes.

with an expedition that was staffed by about 300 soldiers and twice that many Indian servants.

Coronado became the first European to lead an expedition into the interior of the American West, although other individuals — notably those who brought back the stories of the seven cities and Father de Niza — had been there before.

Although he had heard about it, Coronado failed to reach the great trading center in the middle of what is now New Mexico, later known by the Spanish name Gran Quivera. Uninhabited since the late seventeenth century, Gran Quivera was the key point of contact between the Native Americans of the Southwest and the Plains tribes at the time Coronado visited the region.

Coronado did, however, reach the Plains. He got as far north as Nebraska and had contact with the Arapaho, Caddo, Cheyenne, Comanche, Kiowa and perhaps the Dakota (Sioux) people. The members of Coronado's expedition were probably the first Europeans to see buffalo, which he called "hump-backed cattle."

Coronado met with Native Americans who lived in large permanent cities and he met nomadic Native Americans who lived in cone-shaped buffalo-hide houses called tepees, but he found no cities of gold and he was disappointed. In retrospect, the seven cities of Cibola were probably the Rio Grande pueblos with the brilliant late afternoon sun illuminating them as though they were made of gold!

*Above:* Natacka Kachina dancers involved in a Hopi ceremony at Walpi, Arizona in 1893. Kachinas are symbolic of spirits which represent various aspects of Native American cosmology. The Kachina ceremonial cycle lasts from the winter solstice to the summer solstice.

*Above right:* Many of the structures at the Acoma Pueblo in New Mexico are several hundred years old.

*Right:* The house of the governor at the Hopi Pueblo of Shipaulovi on Arizona's Second Mesa, as photographed by William Henry Jackson in 1875. Though more than a century separates the photographs on this page, little has changed over the years.

The northernmost of the pueblos, at Taos, is one of the largest, and to this day, one of the best preserved. Another, the "Sky City" at Acoma near Albuquerque, was over 900 years old in Coronado's time and is the oldest continuously-inhabited city in what is now the United States.

One of Coronado's most important contributions, from the point of view of the Native Americans themselves, was that he was the first to bring horses to the American West.

These animals were unknown to Native Americans, but as horses were either abandoned by or stolen from the Spaniards, they quickly came to be adopted as a vital element in the culture and lifestyle of the Indians of the American West.

The Spanish returned to the Rio Grande Valley to establish trading posts and missions in 1598. Despite Coronado's earlier visit, the Pueblos welcomed the Spanish under Juan de Onate, because they hoped that Spain would help to shield them from Apache and Navajo raiders. However, in 1680, the Pueblos revolted against the Spanish settlers, forcing them out. In 1693, Diego de Vargas returned to reestablish Spanish colonial rule, although relations with the native people would gradually improve.

In 1821, when Mexico became independent of Spain, it inherited control of the Pueblos, and, in 1846, the United States gained jurisdiction of the area after the Mexican War. A year later, the Pueblos again revolted, but again they were subjugated. When the Bureau of Indian Affairs began establishing reservations after 1853, each of the 19 pueblos — along with the surrounding land — were recognized as a reservation.

Today, each pueblo has its own tribal government, traditions and ceremonies, and exists a sovereign and separate entity. The 19 pueblos are Zuni, 154 miles west of Albuquerque; Acoma, 64 miles west of Albuquerque; Laguna, 47 miles west of

*Above:* A Hopi woman making a pot, circa 1910. The Native Americans of the Southwest, notably the Hopi, are famous for the quality of their pottery work.

Albuquerque; Isleta, 15 miles south of Albuquerque; Sandia, 13 miles north of Albuquerque; Santa Ana, 26 miles north of Albuquerque; Zia, 34 miles north of Albuquerque; Jemez, 45 miles north of Albuquerque; San Felipe, 28 miles north of Albuquerque; Santo Domingo, 38 miles north of Albuquerque; Cochiti, 47 miles north of Albuquerque; Tesuque, nine miles north of Santa Fe; Pojoaque, 15 miles north of Santa Fe; San Ildefonso, 21 miles north of Santa Fe; Nambe, 18 miles north of Santa Fe; Santa Clara, 25 miles north of Santa Fe; San Juan, 29 miles north of Santa Fe; Picuris, 57 miles north of Santa Fe; and Taos, 73 miles north of Santa Fe.

The Pueblos typically welcome visitors and much can be learned about Native American culture by visiting the Pueblos, especially during the specific dances and feast days open to the public.

While the Pueblos are generally receptive to visitors, they are also very careful to guard the sanctity of their centuries-old cities, and recognize that events such as their dances, are religious in nature and not staged performances. The Pueblos all promote cultural relations with the outside world through their Pueblo Cultural Center, located in Albuquerque.

*Below:* A "beehive" oven at the Acoma Pueblo in New Mexico. Acoma, known as "Sky City," is located on a mesa top. The land in the distance is owned by the people of the pueblo and used for farming and grazing.

*Above:* A winter view of the Taos Pueblo is included in this series of historic and contemporary photographs of the New Mexico pueblos.

*Top right:* The kiva, or semi-subterranean ceremonial chamber at the Cochiti Pueblo, circa 1911.

*Right:* A view of the Laguna Pueblo today, with the white-washed church prominent on the skyline.

*Below:* Participants in a corn dance at Santa Clara Pueblo, circa 1911.

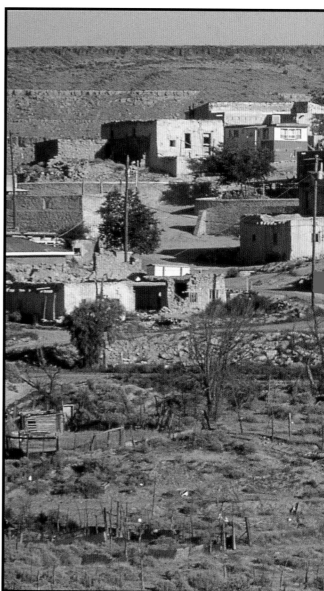

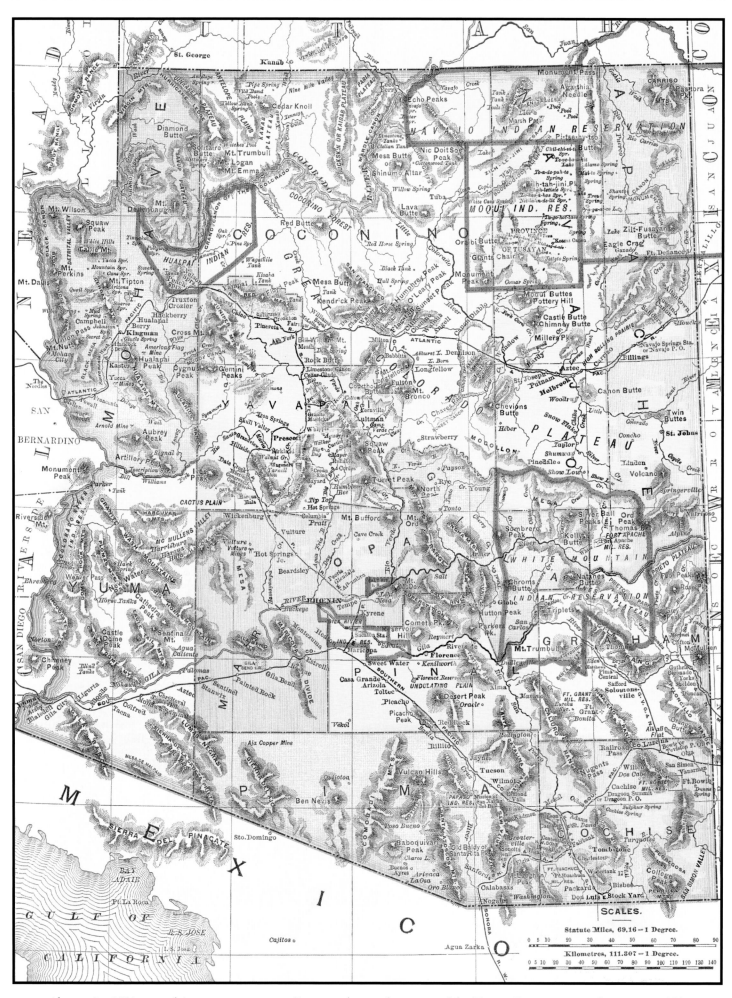

*Above:* An 1891 map of Arizona reservations. Compare this configuration of the Navajo Reservation to that on page 108.

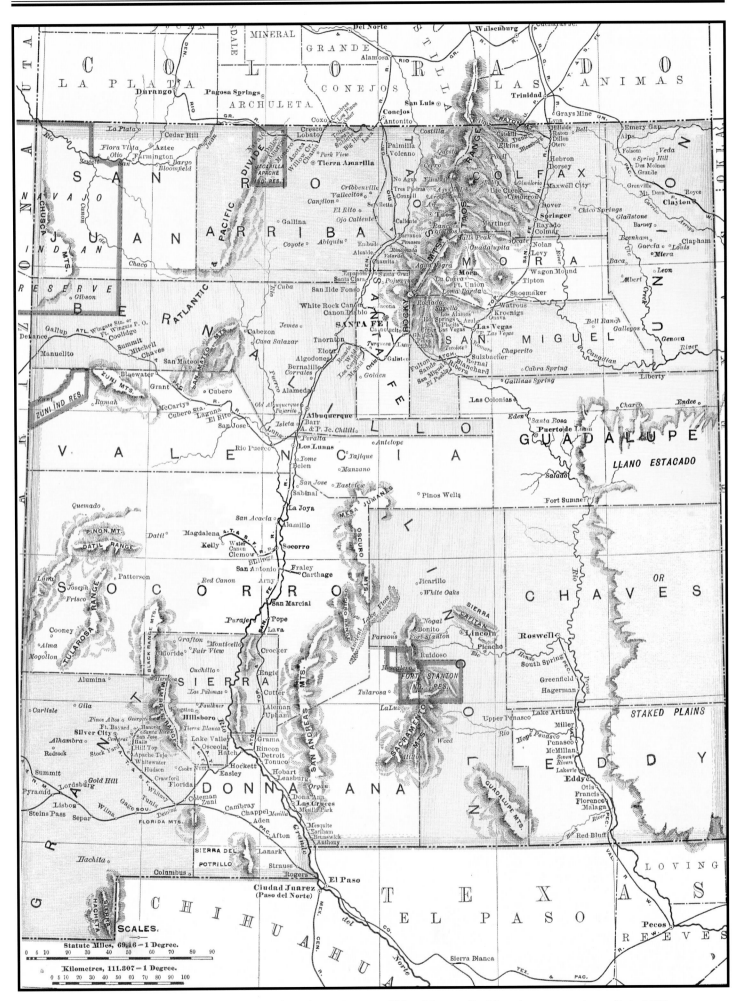

*Above:* Not all of the pueblos appeared on this 1891 map of New Mexico. Pueblo culture was at its nadir in 1891.

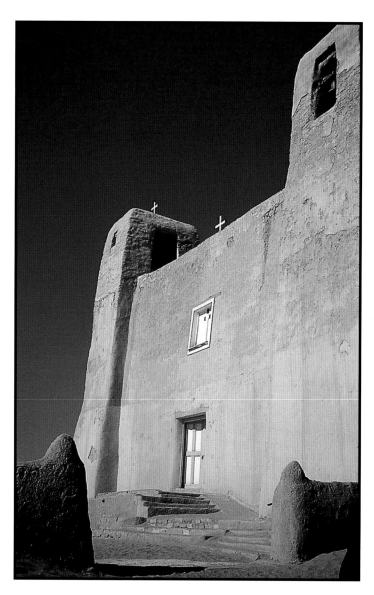

*Above:* Constructed in 1629, the old Spanish church of San Esteban del Rey (St. Stephen the King) at the Acoma Pueblo is still used on a regular basis. The native peoples of the pueblos adopted many aspects of Catholicism without abandoning all aspects of their own indigenous culture.

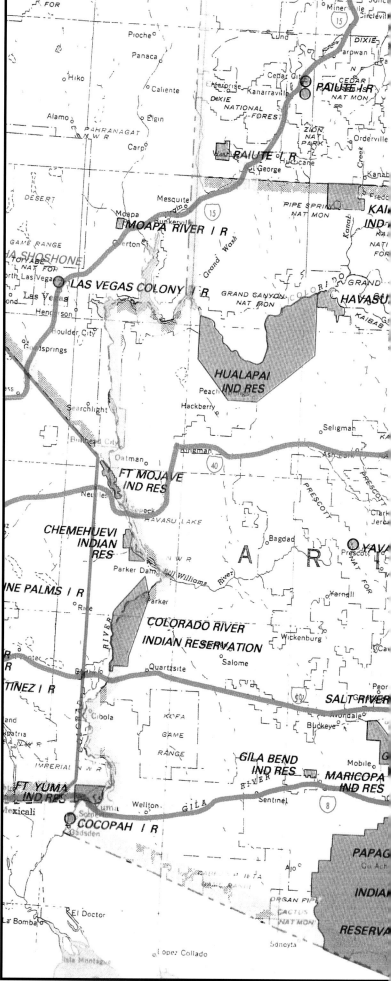

*Right:* This contemporary map of Southwest reservations includes the Hopi Reservation, the sprawling Navajo Reservation, several Apache reservations and all the pueblos in New Mexico.

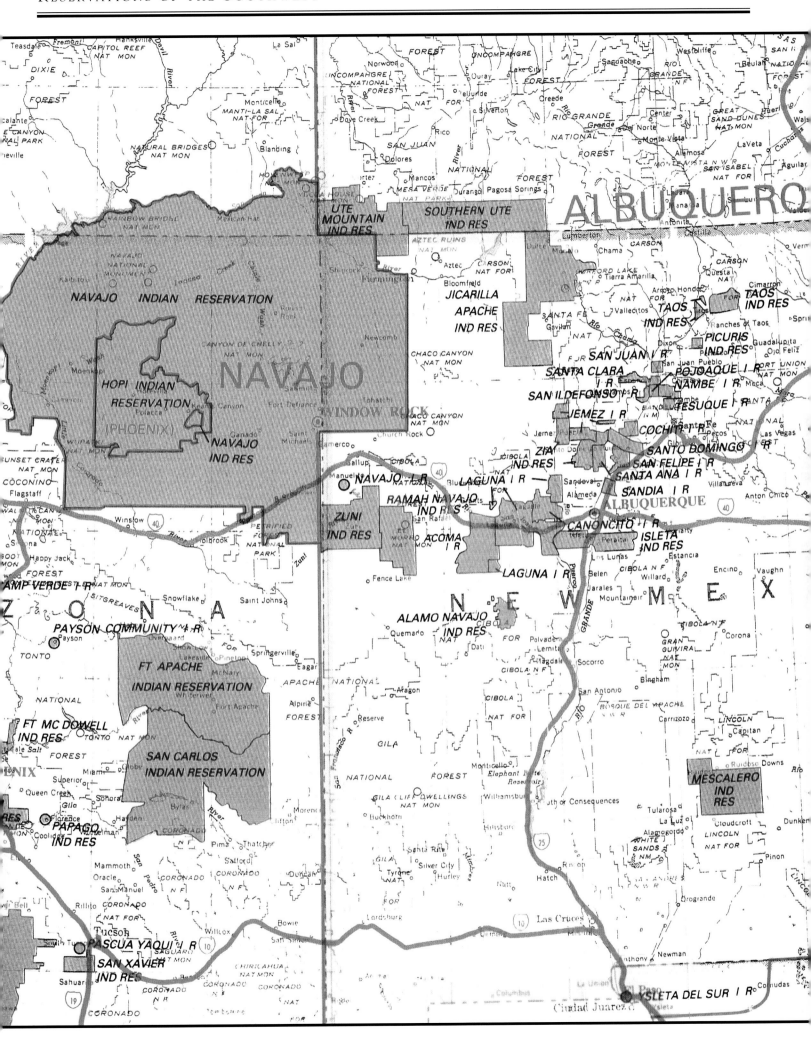

# FIRST NATIONS OF CANADA

Historically, the relations between the native people of Canada and the government of Canada were generally marked by less hostility and confrontation than were the parallel relations in the United States. Canada never had an outright Indian War, although the Northwest Rebellions of 1869-1870 and 1884-1885, led by Louis Riel, were significant uprisings. Still, the British colonial authority of Canada did not seek the level of westward expansion and exploration that the United States government so readily embraced. Yet it should also be acknowledged that the struggle for recognition and autonomy for the Indians of Canada has been and remains a pressing issue.

As noted earlier, the equivalent of the United States Bureau of Indian Affairs in Canada is the Department of Indian and Northern Affairs (DINA). Since the early 1980s, Canadian Indians have formed 633 communities known as "First Nations" throughout Canada. The Assembly of First Nations (formerly the National Indian Brotherhood) is a First Nations institution where the leaders of tribal governments assemble to devise common strategies on collective issues.

The Assembly of First Nations exists to fulfill the goal of correcting past injustices and to enhance the rightful position of the First Nations Peoples in Canada's future. Considering the short time that the Assembly of First Nations has been in existence, significant progress has been made in the Canadian political arena. The Assembly of First Nations is structured so as to present the views of various First Nations through their leaders in areas such as aboriginal and treaty rights, environment, economic development, education, housing, health, social services, land claims, and other issues of common concern.

Although the First Nations Peoples of Canada are identified in the Constitution as one of the founding nations of Canada (along with the English and French), the struggle for Canadian native political identity has been just as complex as in the United States.

Although it is not widely known, until the First Ministers Conference on Aboriginal Rights in the 1983 to 1987 period, the people of Canada's First Nations were excluded from taking part in the Constitutional developments of Canada.

Like Indians in America who witnessed the loss of their land and a way of life, First Nations Peoples have had to deal with conditions of extreme poverty and isolation, and vast geographical dispersion, within the tremendous diversity of aboriginal cultures, languages and political ideologies. Governmental acts (such as the 1927 Indian Act) forbade First Nations Peoples from forming political organizations and from speaking their native languages. However, recent activism has attempted to earn them their rightful place in contemporary Canada. Improved communications and transportation have allowed First Nations Peoples to begin to talk to each other, to the rest of Canada and to the rest of the world. These relatively recent developments

*Right:* This Haida totem, from the west coast of British Columbia, represents a bear.

have meant that the First Nations Peoples have had to work harder and faster in order to catch up with the federal and provincial governments in the fields of political knowledge, political reality, and political expertise.

One of the first attempts at forming a national presence for First Nations came soon afterthe First World War. During this time, The League of Nations was formed. The League of Indians in Canada was also established, but like The League of Nations it failed to attract widespread support, and often faced Canadian government actions that were suppressive and detrimental to their early goals and actions. The League of Indians in Canada soon faded from the national scene.

After the Second World War, First Nations again attempted to form a national lobby group. The North American Indian Brotherhood (NAIB) was established in the late 1940s, but, like its predecessor, the NAIB's efforts were hindered by a lack of nationwide support, as well as government actions, especially in the province of Saskatchewan, where the Cooperative Commonwealth Federation government was seen as working against First Nations initiatives. Furthermore, internal administrative problems caused the organization to break into regional factions, causing the NAIB to disband during the early 1950s.

During the next ten years, First Nations began to reorganize their efforts to form a new national lobby group. In 1961, the National Indian Council was formed to represent three of the four major groups of aboriginal people in Canada. They are as follows: Treaty and Status people; the Non-status people; and the Metis people (the Inuit were excluded).

*Above:* Assiniboine people at a trading post on the Canadian Prairie, circa 1890.

Thus, since 1961, the First Nations of Canada have always had a national lobby group to represent them in Ottawa. The stated purpose of the National Indian Council was to promote "unity among all Indian people."

However, the National Indian Council found the task of uniting all of the various First Nations Peoples' interests into one national lobby to be rather difficult. Also, as the various First Nations became more articulate in their demands, they found less and less in common with each other. This disunity led to the National Indian Council splitting up, by mutual agreement of the three aboriginal groups, in 1968. The Status and Treaty aboriginal groups formed the National Indian Brotherhood, while the Non-status and the Metis groups remained united and formed the Native Council of Canada.

The National Indian Brotherhood (NIB) was born in the midst of controversy. Soon after the brotherhood came into existence, the Federal Liberal Government revealed its 1969 White Paper policy, which called for the assimilation of all First Nation Peoples into the mainstream of Canadian society, and the removal of First Nations from the Canadian Constitution.

The National Indian Brotherhood quickly organized itself and confronted the Liberal government. With the unity of its provincial and territorial members, the National Indian

*Below:* A group of Hamatsa, or elders, of the Kwakiutl tribe attending a feast at Fort Rupert on Vancouver Island, British Columbia, circa 1894.

Brotherhood successfully lobbied Parliament and the Canadian public to defeat the White Paper. For the next 13 years, the National Indian Brotherhood's structure remained relatively unchanged, with the provincial and territorial organizations forming its major pillars of strength.

Over the years, the National Indian Brotherhood became an ever-present watchdog agency, as well as a means for First Nations to press for changes in federal and provincial aboriginal policies. The solid research and careful application of political pressure has resulted in many changes in federal and provincial aboriginal policies.

Despite the success of the National Indian Brotherhood, problems were apparent. Organizing all the various status First Nations groups across Canada into a single, cohesive lobby group still presented the biggest difficulty. The National Indian Brotherhood drew an increasing amount of criticism for not being truly representative of all the status First Nations in the country. The issue slowly rose to the forefront in 1979, and culminated in the arrival of 300 status First Nations and Chiefs in London, England, in an attempt to halt the repatriation of the Canadian Constitution. The Constitution repatriation battle, in England and Canada, was soon reflected internally at the National Indian Brotherhood. The basic structure of the National Indian Brotherhood was in flux and in need of change.

Just as the people of the First Nations across Canada were becoming familiar with the National Indian Brotherhood and its role in serving the status aboriginal people, an important transition in the structure of the secretariat was being discussed, and eventually the chiefs wanted to develop an organization which was truly representative and accountable to their community members; thus the National Indian Brotherhood made the transition to becoming the Assembly of First Nations in 1982.

During those years, the National Indian Brotherhood underwent a drastic revision of its basic structure. With this revision came the name change to the Assembly of First Nations (AFN). From being an "organization of representatives from regions," the Assembly of First Nations became an "organization of First Nations government leaders."

The secretariat of the NIB/AFN became more directly responsible to the First Nations Chiefs-in-Assembly, who were themselves responsible to their First Nations communities. Hence, the NIB/AFN became a truly representative body of the Status and Treaty First Nations Peoples in Canada, and at the same time, a consensus driver. The Assembly of First Nations secretariat serves as the administrative body to the Assembly of First Nations, and under this structure, First Nations government leaders are able to directly formulate and administer the policies of the Assembly of First Nations.

*Above:* An Assiniboine woman, Irene Rock, at her home, circa 1907. Until the twentieth century, the southern part of Saskatchewan was a district of the Northwest Territories known as Assiniboia.

*Right:* An Assiniboine man on horseback, circa 1907.

# THE NATIVE PEOPLE OF THE FAR NORTH

For many years, the people who inhabit the thousands of miles of Arctic coastline in Alaska and northern Canada were called "Eskimo," a name — implying that they ate raw meat — that was given to them by the Athapaskan people to the south. Today, these northern peoples are referred to as "Inuit," the Inuktitut word for "the people."

Inuit primarily live in Alaska, Canada's Northwest Territories and parts of Labrador and Northern Quebec. They have traditionally lived in the area bordered by the Mackenzie Delta in the west, the Labrador coast in the east, the southern point of Hudson Bay in the south, and the High Arctic islands in the north.

Despite the vast changes Inuit culture has undergone in the past century, fundamental Inuit values and culture have been maintained. Inuktitut is still spoken in all Inuit communities and is used in several northern newspapers and television stations. The principal food source is still marine mammals, and animal skins are still used as a source of clothing: caribou skins for parkas and leggings, seal skin for boots, and furs for hoods on parkas. Today, elected municipal governments with a mayor and council govern most Inuit communities. Committees for education, health, hunting, fishing, and trapping oversee the running of community services.

Approximately 55,700 Inuit live in 53 communities across the north of Canada, while the Inuit and Aleut population of Alaska is estimated at 70,000, out of a state-wide native population of over 163,000.

Since the mid-1970s, Inuit have negotiated a number of comprehensive land claims with the Canadian federal government, the Government of the Northwest Territories, and the Province of Quebec. Each agreement meets the needs of the specific region and can include financial compensation, land rights, hunting and trapping rights, participation in land and resource management, and economic development opportunities.

The James Bay and Northern Quebec Agreement (JBNQA), signed in 1975, was the first comprehensive claim to be settled in Canada. It was followed by the Northeastern Quebec Agreement (NEQA), which was signed in 1978. Together these agreements gave the 19,000 Cree, Inuit, and Naskapi of Northern Quebec more than $230 million in compensation, ownership over 14,000 square kilometers of territory, and exclusive hunting and trapping rights over another 150,000 square kilometers.

The Inuvialuit Final Agreement with 2,500 Inuvialuit (Inuit living in the Western Arctic) was signed in 1984. The settlement provided them with 91,000 square kilometers of land; $152 million over 13 years; guaranteed hunting and trapping rights and equal participation in the management of wildlife, conservation, and the environment; a $10 million Economic Enhancement Fund; and a $7.5 million Social Development Fund.

Alaska's 70,000 Inuit, Indian and Aleut aboriginal people live in more than 240 villages, as well as in the state's major cities. They are found in Kaktovik and

*Right:* A pair of happy Inuit children.

Barrow on the Arctic Ocean coast, in Atka and Akutan on islands in the Aleutians, on the Pribilof Islands of St. Paul and St. George in the Bering Sea, in the tundra communities of Tuntutu-liak and Mountain Village on the Yukon and Kuskokwim River deltas, and in forested communities such as Hydaburg and Angoon in the southeast panhandle area.

Distance and remoteness take on new meaning in Alaska. There is no state-wide network of roads. Access to most native communities is only by air or water. Living in rural Alaska some-times requires innovation and a helping hand. For many coastal villages that helping hand has been a succession of ships named *North Star*.

Bureau of Indian Affairs activities in Alaska began in 1884, when the Secretary of the Interior, under the territory's First Organic Act, was made responsible for education. Sheldon Jackson, a Presbyterian missionary, was appointed General Agent for Education in 1884. In the 1890s, Jackson purchased and had shipped to the northwest coast a herd of Siberian reindeer. He expected the animals to provide an alternate food source and a cash "crop." Jackson's original herd was few in number, but today

*Below:* Inuit woman with a basket, photographed in Kotzebue, Alaska. Alaskan natives live in villages rather than on reservations.

there are more than 20,000 animals in about 20 herds in such varied locations as Atka in the Aleutians, Nunivak and Hage-meister Islands, and the Seward Peninsula. Sales of reindeer products for cash have included the horns as well as the hides. The meat has been sold, as well as processed for personal consumption.

Reindeer also provided work in an area of severe unemployment in 1983 and 1984. Jobs Bill funds were used for construction of reindeer corrals on the Seward Peninsula. Most of the money was used for wages, since available driftwood constituted the raw materials.

The Bureau of Indian Affairs' role in Alaska is continually changing. Where the bureau once provided almost all direct services, a growing state government is expanding its delivery systems. Bureau services, designed for delivery on reserva-tions in the contiguous United States, are available to each Alaska native. However, where bureau activities have duplicated those of state efforts, the bureau defers to the state.

At one time the bureau operated 137 day schools and three boarding schools in Alaska, but in the early 1960s, as the state

*Above:* This selection of Alaskan native crafts includes an Inuit mask and carvings, as well as items related to the Tlingit people.

*Right:* An Inuit man having a successful day of ice fishing.

education system matured, the bureau entered an agreement with the state to gradually turn schools over to the state system.

In 1982 the bureau operated 37 village schools and one boarding high school, Mt. Edgecumbe at Sitka. At the end of that school year, 17 of the village schools were transferred to the state system. Congress then directed, in the 1983 appropriation bill, that Mt. Edgecumbe be closed or transferred to the state in 1983 and that the remaining 20 village schools be transferred to the state before the 1985-1986 school year.

A profound change in the Alaska scene has occurred as a result of the Alaska Native Claims Settlement Act, (ANCSA) passed in 1971. The act served to settle a variety of native claims by providing for transfer to the natives of 44 million acres of land and almost $1 billion. Thirteen regional and more than 200 village native corporations were created to receive and administer tribal lands and funds for eligible Alaska native shareholders. These village corporations also provide a vehicle for contracting services on behalf of village residents from both state and federal programs.

Passage of the Alaska Native Claims Settlement Act in 1971 gained for the natives a land base and a start at business experience. Passage of the Indian Self-Determination and Education Assistance Act in 1975 created a means for greater native control and decision-making in those activities that affect them.

ANCSA set aside two million acres of land to be conveyed to Alaska natives in various other categories. The bureau has been active in the past few years locating and identifying cemetery sites and historic places, traditional lands used by native groups, and native primary places of residence. A total of 500,000 acres can be conveyed to natives in these categories. In all cases, once the Bureau of Indian Affairs has completed its work, another Interior Department agency, the Bureau of Land Management, completes necessary surveys and conveyance documents.

*Above:* A group of young Tlingits in traditional costume. The Tlingit live in southeastern Alaska, known as the "panhandle."

Individual natives have, since 1906, been eligible to apply for 160-acre allotments of land. Although few applications were processed before the mid-1970s, there has been considerable effort to identify and complete processing on all allotment applications filed before the 1971 deadline.

By the end of 1983, about 640 individual allotments, representing some 67,000 acres, had been conveyed to Alaska natives or their heirs. Remaining to be completed are about 8,500 applications representing 1.3 million acres.

## THE NUNAVUT AGREEMENT

One of the most striking developments in recent Canadian native history is the landmark Nunavut Land Claims Agreement, reached with the Tungavik Federation of Nunavut. Finalized in 1993, it is the largest comprehensive claim in Canada. The agreement will provide some 17,500 Inuit of the Eastern Arctic with

*Below:* These two Tlingit women and their children were photographed at Kotsina River, Alaska by the Miles Brothers in 1902.

350,000 square kilometers of land, financial compensation of $1.17 billion over 14 years, the right to share in resource royalties and hunting rights, and a greater role in the management of land and the environment. The final agreement committed the federal government to a process to divide the Northwest Territories and create the new territory of Nunavut in 1999.

The word "Nunavut" is an Inuktitut word for "our land." In 1976 the Inuit Tapirisat of Canada (ITC), a national Inuit organization, proposed that a new territory in northern Canada be created. The new territory, called Nunavut, would include the central and eastern area of the Northwest Territories, where the majority of residents are Inuit.

In 1990, the federal government asked John Parker, former Commissioner of the Northwest Territories, to recommend a single-line boundary between the claims settlement areas of the Dene/Meacutetis and the Inuit. This boundary was presented to all Northwest Territories voters as the jurisdictional boundary for division in a May 1992 plebiscite. Of those voting, 54 percent supported the proposed boundary. The Government of the Northwest Territories, the Tungavik Federation of Nunavut and the Canadian federal government formally adopted the boundary for division in the Nunavut Political Accord.

An Agreement-in-Principle to settle the Nunavut Land Claim Agreement was finalized in April 1990. A provision of this affirmed federal, territorial and Inuit support for the creation of Nunavut "as soon as possible." This article also provided a process, separate from the claims negotiations, to further this objective.

In December 1991, negotiations were finalized on outstanding items in the land claim, including the creation of Nunavut. The final agreement committed Canada and the government of the Northwest Territories to negotiate a political accord (separate from the land claim settlement) to deal with powers, principles of financing and timing for the establishment of a

*Below:* An Inuit woman in front of a traditional hide-covered home, circa 1935.

distinct Nunavut government. This political accord was formally signed on October 30, 1992.

The Inuit ratification vote for the land claim settlement agreement was held November 3-5, 1992. Sixty-nine percent of eligible Inuit voters cast ballots. Of those who voted, 85 percent approved the claim settlement. Government and Inuit representatives signed the land claim agreement on May 25, 1993.

The Nunavut Territory and government, established effective April 1, 1999, is a jurisdiction with powers and institutions similar to those of the territorial governments.

As part of the Nunavut public government, there will be an elected Legislative Assembly, a Cabinet, a territorial court and a Nunavut public service. The Nunavut Act, which received Royal Assent on June 10, 1993, establishes the legal framework for the new government.

*Below:* An Inuit couple in traditional parkas at Kotzebue, Alaska, circa 1990.

*Above:* A traditional Chilkat ceremonial dance being performed in Alaska.

*Left:* The traditional Inuit blanket toss is exciting to watch, but not half as exciting as it is for the participant.

*Above:* Tlingit artist Nathan Jackson at work on a totem pole at his studio in Ketchikan in southeastern Alaska.

*Right:* An Inuit family sits for a group portrait by William Dinwiddie, in Port Clarence, Alaska, circa 1894.

# THE GAMING DEBATE

The reservation experience of many Indians in the United States during the recessions of the 1970s led to a period of an undeniable uncertainty about the future. Reservation life quietly went on. Problems such as poverty and unemployment failed to go away. Indians continued the balancing act they'd been doing ever since their constriction to reservation life that began in the mid-nineteenth century — that is, maintaining their traditions and beliefs while also dealing with the dominant white culture and economic realities.

The activism surrounding the Red Power movement of the 1960s and 1970s briefly brought some attention to the plight of reservation life. Counterculture figures and young hippies adopted many Native American beliefs, including the importance of living off the land and cultivating a harmonious relationship between nature and humanity.

Another segment of the American population demonstrated an interest in Indian art, crafts, jewelry, literature, culture and history. Later, the emergence of the "New Age" movement would be criticized by some for appropriating Native American religious beliefs for profit. But for the most part, the Native American remained relegated to reservation life at the margins of mainstream American society. During the 1980s, however, that was to change. Indians and the reservation system in general were thrust into the national spotlight over the controversial issue of gaming.

A major economic surge on Indian reservations occurred in 1983 with the sudden growth of bingo games, which brought a great deal of needed revenue into tribal coffers. About a dozen tribes followed the lead of the Seminole tribe in Florida, offering high-stake games with prizes amounting to thousands of dollars. Another 50 or 60 tribes initiated or expanded smaller games with success. Court rulings had made it clear that tribes on reservations are not subject to state civil and regulatory laws, which limit the scope of bingo operations in most states.

Some Indian bingo games attracted busloads of players — including those from nearby states — to the reservations. On one reservation, $1 million in prizes was awarded in a single day. A few tribes have discussed building entertainment centers with hotels, restaurants and shops. In most cases, bingo did bring income to the reservation economy. It also created jobs for tribal members. On many reservations, bingo profits were soon being used to fund tribal social programs and other tribal governmental operations.

A report from one reservation said bingo "has created 100 percent employment, has improved the standard of living and has made funds available for community improvement, health and education. It has created less reliance on federal funds and enabled the concept of self-determination to be more fully realized by the tribe."

*Right:* Tunica-Biloxi tribal member Anna Juneau with a guest at the Grand Casino Avoyelles in Marksville, Louisiana.

While the bingo movement of the early 1980s was perceived as a positive step from a tribal point of view, it brought complaints from segments of the non-Indian community. Indian bingo, it was said, deprived churches and non-Indian charity groups from raising much-needed funds with their own bingo games. Also, there was the possibility of organized crime involvement in the high stakes Indian games. Opponents to Indian bingo argued that Indians should be subject to state regulations like anyone else.

A Bureau of Indian Affairs task force on bingo was established, but it was later changed to a tribal task force at the request of the tribes. Made up of nine tribal leaders and one Interior official, who served as an observer, the tribal task force worked to address problems related to the bingo issue. It also worked to protect the authority of tribal governments to stage games, maintain jobs and plan for use of the income bingo brings.

Meanwhile, there were efforts being made which would lead to the establishment of full-scale casino gaming on Indian reservations. Prior to 1988, legalized forms of gaming existed in only two states, Nevada and New Jersey. However, that was the year in which Congress passed the Indian Gaming Regulatory Act,

*Above:* Many Tunica-Biloxi tribal members are employed at the Grand Casino Avoyelles in Marksville, Louisiana. They are known as "associates" rather than "employees," and over 95 percent reside in Avoyelles Parish. The casino was opened in 1994 under the leadership of Tribal Chairman Earl Barbry, Sr., Profits have allowed the tribe to invest in other types of businesses.

*Above:* Anna Juneau displays a selection of Tunica-Biloxi crafts at the Grand Casino Avoyelles. The casino complex also includes a separate tribal museum.

which recognized the right of Indian tribes in the United States to establish gaming and gaming facilities on their reservations as long as the states in which they are located have some form of legalized gaming. In addition, the Indian Gaming Regulatory Act ensures that the federal government maintains its position of supremacy over tribes and tribal/state relations.

Two important cases in the 1980s led up to the passage of the act, Seminole Tribe of Florida v. Butterworth and California v. Cabazon Band of Mission Indians. The Seminole case had opened the doors to high-stakes bingo on reservations all over the country. Florida tried to close the Seminole tribe's high-stakes bingo parlor — which had opened in 1979 — but the court ruled that bingo fell under statutes classed as regulatory rather than prohibitory. The Cabazon case established that once a state has legalized any form of gaming, Indian tribes within that state can offer the same game on trust land without any state interference or restrictions. Trust land is reserved for and owned by Indians but held "in trust" by the federal government for the benefit of the Indian owners.

The act officially went into effect on October 17, 1988, intending to:

1. Promote tribal economic development, self-sufficiency and strong tribal government.

2. Provide for a regulatory base to protect Indian gaming from organized crime.

3. Establish the National Indian Gaming Commission.

Beyond this, the act defines three classes of gaming:

- Class I: Social games solely for prizes of minimal value or traditional forms of Indian gaming engaged in by individuals as a part of, or in connection with, tribal ceremonies or celebrations.
- Class II: All forms of bingo, and other games similar to bingo, such as pull tabs, lotto, etc., and card games that are explicitly authorized by state law, not including blackjack, baccarat, or chemin de fer.
- Class III: All forms of gaming that are not Class I gaming or Class II gaming. States have no power to tax, regulate, or police casinos run by Indian tribes.

Indian gaming revenues are also exempt from federal, state, and local taxes. According to statistics from the National Gaming Association, 90 of the nation's 557 tribes were involved in gaming by the late 1990s, and Native American gaming operations accounted for approximately 200 gaming sites in 19 states.

Just as the advent of gaming on reservations sparked heated debate, among both Indians and non-Indians, there were also

*Above:* The dramatic entrance to the Grand Casino Mille Lacs, near Vineland, Minnesota. The revenues from the casino, which opened in April 1991, have allowed the Mille Lacs Band to open two new schools on their 4,039-acre reservation.

*Above:* Fans enjoy some horse racing action at the Fort McDowell Casino on the Fort McDowell Mohave-Apache Indian Reservation. The reservation is located in Maricopa County, Arizona, east of Phoenix.

regulatory discussions at the state and federal levels of government. Arguing that gaming provides a much needed source of revenue and employment, many Native Americans have embraced the advent of casinos and cardhouses as a viable means of economic development for reservations. Gaming advocates point to drops in unemployment and welfare rates and increased funds for tribes as tangible benefits for Native Americans. Indeed, reservation gaming has become not only a way for tribes to assert their autonomy, but a lucrative industry as well. In fact, the Foxwoods High Stakes Bingo and Casino of Ledyard, Connecticut, operated by the Mashantucket Pequot tribe, is believed to be the most profitable casino in the Western Hemisphere.

By 1995, total revenues from Indian gaming had topped the $6 billion mark, with total profits exceeding $1 billion. According to JoAnn Jones, tribal chair of the Wisconsin Winnebago Nation, "The national prominence of tribal casinos has also given Indian leaders potential political clout, especially with the federal government. Tribal governments realize that a casino is not an end in itself. It is a means to achieve what no state or federal economic development program has been able to achieve for Indian people in 200 years — the return of self-respect and economic self-sufficiency."

Not all Indians, however, have given their blessing to these gaming activities. Besides concerns over potential gaming addiction and an impoverished population spending much needed money on gambling, some Indians (especially elders) fear losing their traditional values to corruption and organized crime. One leader has gone so far as to term gaming "a spiritual cancer eating away at what is left of the soul of Native American communities."

A well known 1990 incident involving the Mohawk on the Akwesasne reservation — which is located inside the New York state, Quebec, and Ontario borders along the St. Lawrence River near Cornwall, Ontario — illustrates this division. The dispute involved six gaming casinos along Route 37, a New York highway. The casinos were illegal under New York law, but their operators insisted that they were on sovereign territory. The confrontation between the pro- and anti-gaming Mohawk factions reached the point of violence and the use of firearms. The fighting reached its peak when two lives were taken, a Mohawk from each side of the dispute.

*Above:* Happy winners at the Fort McDowell Casino in Arizona. A 1994 expansion more than tripled the size of the facility, and revenues have allowed construction of a tribal cultural center.

Opposition to gaming has not only come from Indians. Since its passage, the Indian Gaming Regulatory Act has also led to a rise of intergovernmental conflicts between the tribes and states over issues involving state sovereignty, criminal jurisdiction, and gaming revenues. States such as Kansas, Oklahoma and Washington have made attempts to block federally required gaming compacts. Other state governments have avoided signing such compacts with tribes by invoking the 10th and 11th Amendments. (The 10th asserts a state's sovereignty and its freedom from being told what to do by Congress. The 11th protects states from being sued.)

Other courts have allowed Indians to offer games that are not permitted anywhere else in the state. For example, in California, a federal judge allowed tribal casinos to operate video poker and keno. In addition, privately-owned casinos in Atlantic City, Las Vegas and elsewhere have felt threatened by the government-sanctioned Indian casinos — as evidenced by Donald Trump's legal action challenging Indian casinos and gaming. On April 30, 1993, Trump filed a civil suit in United States District Court in Newark, New Jersey against United States Secretary of the Interior Bruce Babbitt, and Tony Hope, chairman of the National Indian Gaming Commission, claiming that the Indian Gaming Regulatory Act is unconstitutional and gives Native Americans preferential treatment and an unfair advantage in acquiring licenses for setting up legal casinos on their land. Hoping to get the Indian Gaming Regulatory Act repealed, Trump went on to testify before a congressional hearing on the subject, stating that organized crime is rampant on Indian reservations.

Gaming has also come to the forefront of Canadian reserves. On December 7, 1995, the British Columbia Gaming Commission announced that for the first time casinos would be allowed on native Indian reserves under an expanded provincial gaming policy that was unveiled in early January 1996. Under an expanded proposed policy, 50 percent of the profits from the new casinos will go to native Indian reserves, with 40 percent going to casino operators and 10 percent to the provincial government.

While gaming has received a great deal of notoriety in recent years, the controversy perhaps can be seen to blur other issues —

more complex, more far reaching and historically rooted — facing the reservations. How does the Indian navigate through the labyrinthine past of broken government promises, failed treaties and land reductions? How does the Indian come to terms with a governmental policy some have termed genocide? How should the Indian strive for autonomy and self-sufficiency, yet still realistically maintain a relationship with the Washington bureaucracy? Should the Indian become more "white" or strive to cultivate a strong sense of Indian identity?

These and other questions have vexed the Indian population for a number of years and will no doubt continue to do so. What is certain, however, is the establishment of the reservation as the "home" of the Indian. In a strange way, reservations have become a last retreat for the Indian and a last chance to preserve their culture. The reservation and reservation-based institutions did not extinguish Indians nor their culture, although at times throughout the 150 year period of reservation history it certainly seemed as if that was possible. Once again, the Indians find themselves performing a familiar and intricate juggling of the old and the new, the white and the Indian.

*Below:* The Grand Casino Mille Lacs offers a 400-seat bingo area. When gaming was introduced on Indian reservations in the 1980s, bingo was the first game.

# BUREAU OF INDIAN AFFAIRS ACTIVITIES

Since it was formed in 1834, the Bureau of Indian Affairs (BIA) has been the United States government agency charged with dealing with the Indian reservations as municipal or administrative entities. Just as the relationship has been redefined and reinvented through the years, so too has the bureau itself evolved. Today, the Bureau of Indian Affairs is still part of the Department of the Interior. Functioning through a three-tier organizational structure, the bureau's central office, or headquarters, operates out of Washington, DC. The second level of administration consists of 12 area offices located throughout the United States; these offices, in turn, oversee certain geographical regions. (The specific tribal groups that are administered by these 12 regions are described in great detail in Appendix I of this book.) The third level is made up of agencies, which provide services to one or more tribes.

The top Indian affairs post in the federal government is the sub-cabinet position of Assistant Secretary for Indian Affairs. Ultimately under the authority of the cabinet-level Interior Secretary, the Assistant Secretary is appointed by the president and confirmed by the United States Senate. Continuing lines of authority extend to the Deputy Assistant Secretary for Operations, to the area directors, and, finally, to the agency superintendents. The only area office to serve a single tribe is the Navajo office, which is located in Window Rock, Arizona. The sprawling Navajo Reservation, containing almost 14 million acres of land in Arizona, New Mexico and Utah, is home to more than 160,000 Native Americans, making the Navajo the largest tribe in the United States. The Eastern area office is headquartered in Washington, DC, and directs bureau operations in New York, Connecticut, Rhode Island, Maine, North Carolina, Louisiana, Mississippi and Florida.

Oklahoma has two area offices, one at Muskogee and one at Anadarko. Muskogee's jurisdiction is limited to tribes in eastern Oklahoma, while Anadarko serves Indians in Kansas and western Oklahoma. The Southwestern states of New Mexico and Arizona each boast an area office, as does California. Albuquerque, New Mexico, has jurisdiction in Colorado and New Mexico, while Phoenix, Arizona, serves 46 reservations and colonies in Arizona, Nevada, Utah and California. Representing the Bureau of Indian Affairs in California, the state with the largest Indian population, is the area office in Sacramento.

The Portland, Oregon, area office is responsible for tribes in the Pacific Northwest states of Oregon, Washington, Idaho, the Flathead Reservation in Montana and the Annette Islands Reserve in Southeast Alaska. Billings, Montana, deals with tribes in Montana and Wyoming. The northernmost area office is Juneau, Alaska, which serves Alaska natives. In the upper Midwest, the Aberdeen, South Dakota, area office controls bureau activities in Nebraska, North Dakota and South Dakota, and the area office in Minneapolis, Minnesota,

*Right:* Chief Thunder Cloud confers with a young visitor to the Mattaponi Reservation in Virginia.

*Above:* A Mississippi Choctaw grandmother dresses the hair of her granddaughter.

*Right:* The current reservations of the Dakotas and the Great Lakes area. Compare these Dakota reservations with those on the 1891 map on pages 42-43 and 46-47.

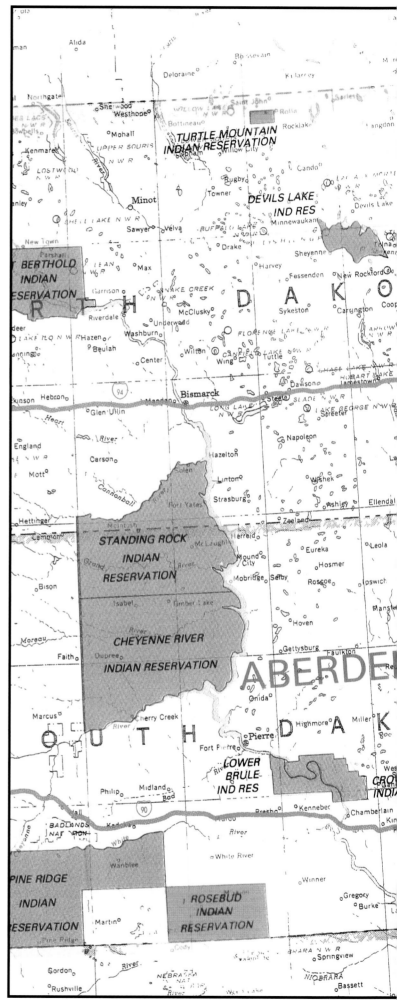

is responsible for the states of Minnesota, Iowa, Michigan and Wisconsin.

There are 84 agency superintendents in the Bureau of Indian Affairs, and theirs is one of the most demanding jobs in the entire federal government. Working directly with tribes on a daily basis, an agency superintendent is concerned with the trust responsibility at its most basic level, and is the essential link in the government-to-government relationship as well. An agency superintendent, by law, has fundamental responsibilities in the proper handling of Native American self-determination contracts and grants.

As tribes become more capable of assuming control of bureau programs, it is the superintendent who works with them to accomplish their goals. Once a contract is entered into, the superintendent is the contracting

*Above:* Though Native Americans living in Maryland, including of Mervyn Savoy, actively celebrate their culture, there are no recognized bands or reservations in the state.

*Right:* The Great Lakes area, primarily under the jurisdiction of the Bureau of Indian Affairs' Minneapolis office, is the location of numerous smaller reservations.

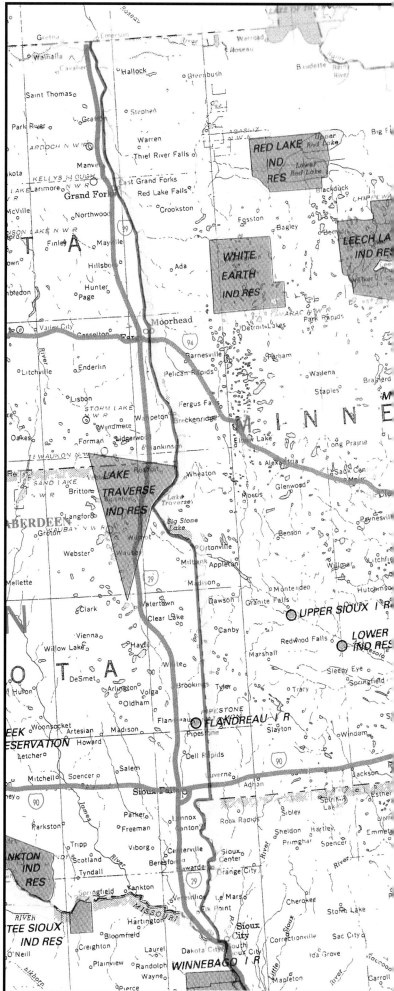

officer's representative, and, as such, is totally responsible for full compliance of the total contract program.

The superintendent also implements bureau policy in other areas and may direct such diverse non-contracted bureau programs as housing, law enforcement, social services, forestry, land operations, tribal operations and roads. He also has fiscal responsibilities to handle the agency budget within stringent regulations.

Added to the degree of difficulty in the superintendent's position is the fact that he may deal with more than one tribe and must relate to each tribe's special problems and varied interests.

The Bureau of Indian Affairs is itself basically Indian. A count made at the end of 1983 showed 15,729 employees on its payroll, and Indians constitute more than 80 percent of the bureau workforce. Preference hiring of Native Americans, which favors the

placement of Indians over non-Indians for employment in the Bureau of Indian Affairs and Indian Health Service, has attracted more Indians to the bureau's labor pool. This policy of Indian preference was controversial when implemented, but it was upheld by the United States Supreme Court in the Mancari v. Morton case in 1974.

Indians hold nearly all of the top management positions in the bureau's central office and 12 area offices. About 90 percent of the organization's agency superintendents are Indian.

*Above:* Dancers prepare for their role in the Seminole Intertribal Pow wow in Oklahoma.

*Right:* The current reservations in Oklahoma are vastly smaller than they were at the turn of the century, especially in the area that was Indian Territory until 1907. Compare this map to the one on pages 20-21. The Osage Reservation, which originated in 1866 as a small slice of the huge Cherokee Nation, is now the largest in Oklahoma.

# PROGRAM SERVICES

In providing services to tribes, the United States federal government and the Bureau of Indian Affairs today assume a role similar to that of municipalities or local governments, which also offer services to their citizens. Most of the programs available from the Bureau of Indian Affairs were initiated in the twentieth century. This is largely a result of the deleterious effect of the General Allotment Act, instituted in 1887, and the changing direction of Indian policy during the administration of Franklin D. Roosevelt.

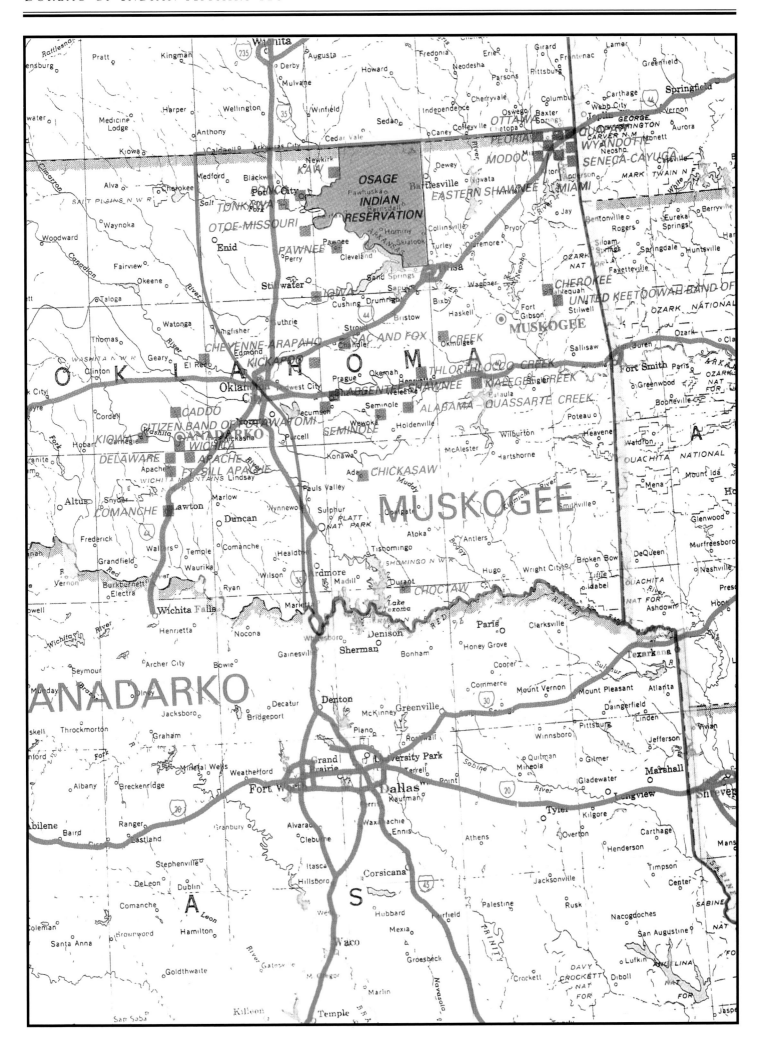

*Above:* A photo by Donnie Sexton of the annual Crow Fair, held at Crow Agency, Montana on the Crow Reservation.

*Right:* Montana has more land area devoted to Indian reservations than any other state except Arizona and South Dakota. The Blackfeet and Flathead have the most people.

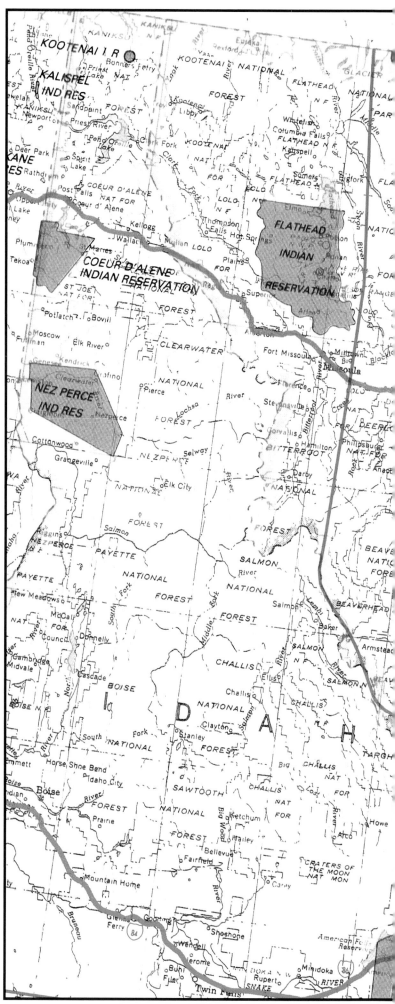

Many different motives have been attributed to the passage of the General Allotment Act. Some point to the desire which existed on the part of non-Indian settlers for more land. There also was a feeling that if tribal governments could be broken up, it would be easier to "civilize" the Native Americans. Certainly there existed a desire to assimilate the Indian into the dominant, non-Indian society.

Whatever the reasons behind it, the allotment policy depleted the economic base of tribes and individual Native Americans and severely curtailed tribal government capabilities. As tribes became more dependent upon the federal government for survival, the federal government responded with added services.

Federal policy in Indian affairs changed, too, paralleling the programs set into motion by the government in Washington for other Americans. As federal involvement in the lives of the citizenry increased with the New Deal of the Roosevelt Administration during the Depression years, Indian policy followed the lead.

As a result, the Bureau of Indian Affairs found itself with programs designed to assist tribes. The Bureau of Indian Affairs was primarily a program services organization until the 1970s, when the push toward self-determination shifted control of many of these programs to the tribes themselves. Through contracting, today it is the tribes, and not the Bureau of Indian Affairs, who operate a large number of programs on the reservations.

The tribal government services program provides funds for community services, fire protection, agricultural extension, tribal enrollment and technical support to tribal government administrative activities. It also provides for the improvement and operation of 119 tribal courts and 19 courts of Indian offenses, which enforce and adjudicate the provisions of tribal law and order codes.

The Bureau of Indian Affairs' housing program is involved with renovation of existing homes to insure decent, safe and sanitary housing for Native American communities. Social services provides general assistance grants to eligible Indians in 14 states. Child welfare assistance provides foster home care and residential care for handicapped children at a rate of 3,000 participants per month on reservations. Bureau of Indian Affairs forestry and fire suppression programs provide forest management services for 13.3 million acres of tribal forest land on 104 reservations in 23 states. Natural resource programs of the Bureau of Indian Affairs provide for the protection, inventory, development and management of Indian natural resources on the 52.2 million acres of lands under the trust responsibility of the Bureau of Indian Affairs. The agricultural program provides technical assistance through agency offices to the Indian reservations for protection and enhancement of 42 million acres of tribal farm and ranch lands. A roads maintenance program provides for the repair and maintenance of 25,600 miles of public roads serving Indian reservations. Bureau of Indian Affairs wildlife and parks programs will support 23 Indian fish hatchery facilities expected to produce and release some 70 million salmon and trout.

*Above:* A happy family of Maryland natives in traditional costume.

*Above:* A pair of young Coushatta dancers ready to participate in the Louisiana Folklife Festival.

The irrigation and power operation and maintenance program assists entitled landowners to conserve water and to properly operate and maintain irrigation water delivery systems on 61 of 70 Indian irrigation projects. The other nine are projects where the assessments are fixed at a rate to return the full operation and maintenance cost. The 70 projects irrigate some 700,000 acres, with a gross crop value estimated in excess of $100 million.

In addition to these services made available to tribes, the Bureau of Indian Affairs also has an administrative division, responsible for providing staff services in support of the organization's management and mission.

## SPECIFIC PROGRAMS

The passage of the Indian Self-Determination and Educational Assistance Act of 1975 greatly facilitated contracting for the operation of educational programs by tribal groups. Three years later, the Educational Amendments Act of 1978 established a new line of authority from the Assistant Secretary to the director of the bureau's education office, and then to the professional educators at the schools and field offices. Implementation of the latter also resulted in decision-making powers for Indian school boards, local hiring of teachers and staff, direct funding to schools, and increased authority for the director of Indian education programs within the Bureau of Indian Affairs.

Education is the largest line item in the entire Bureau of Indian Affairs budget, funding a total of over 200 education facil-

*Above:* A craftswoman at work on the Cherokee Reservation in North Carolina. The Cherokee are the third largest tribe in the United States after the Navajo and Dakota (Sioux).

*Right:* Across the continent, the Pacific Northwest is characterized by large inland reservations and numerous small enclaves along the coast and around Puget Sound.

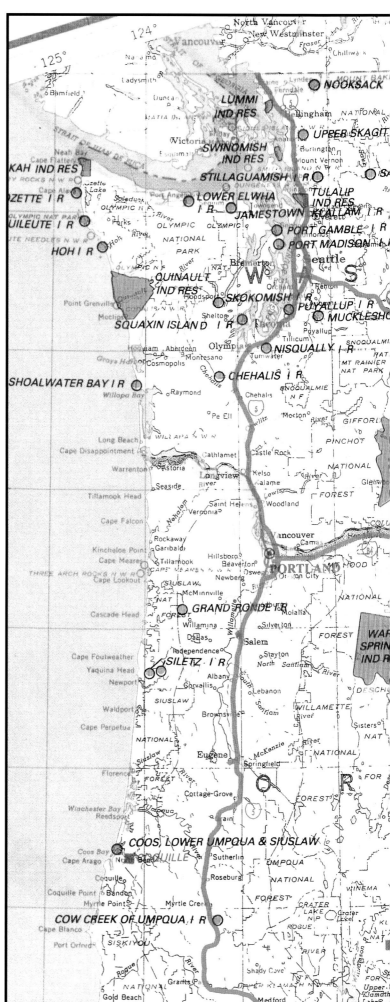

ities, including day schools, on-reservation boarding schools, off-reservation boarding schools and tribally-contracted schools. The need for off-reservation boarding schools has declined with the development of schools on the reservations. The off-reservation schools are underutilized and have become very expensive, per pupil, to keep open.

The Bureau of Indian Affairs also provides funds under the Johnson O'Malley Act of 1934 to meet the special needs of Indian students in public schools. These funds, which are largely administered through contracts with tribal organizations, public school districts and state departments of education, provide supplemental programs for Indian students.

The Bureau of Indian Affairs also provides grants for the operation of tribally-controlled community col-

leges as authorized by the Tribally-Controlled Community College Assistance Act of 1978. The Bureau of Indian Affairs operates post-secondary schools, such as Haskell Indian Junior College in Lawrence, Kansas, which has an enrollment of about 950 students, the Institute of American Indian Arts at Santa Fe, New Mexico, with about 160 students, and Southwestern Polytechnic Institute at Albuquerque, New Mexico, with about 600 students.

In the Yupik-speaking area of Alaska, a bilingual program, conceived as a means of preserving the Inuit language and identity, has turned upside down the traditional methods, which require students to learn solely in English. Under this bilingual concept, students in the program are being taught in tribal dialects, with short periods each day devoted to the study of English, a foreign language to most of them. The objective of the program is to help students in the early grades become literate in both tribal language and English. Each year, English is taught with the emphasis gradually shifting from the tribal language. By the fourth year, students are learning mainly in English.

So successful was the 1970 pilot bilingual program in Alaska, that it is now a part of the Bureau of Indian Affairs education program in many other regions of the country. Of the 50,000 students served in the elementary and secondary education programs of the Bureau of Indian Affairs, more than 7,000 have participated in bilingual programs, helping them to begin the learning process through their native language.

*Below:* The Indian Health Service of the Bureau of Indian Affairs maintains a number of hospitals and clinics, such as this one on the Crow Reservation in Montana.

*Above:* A participant in the annual Crow Fair held on the Crow Reservation. The event is one of the premier native cultural events in eastern Montana.

Computer education, fast becoming a necessity and no longer the wave of the future, has been integrated into the curriculum of many Bureau of Indian Affairs schools, even at the first grade level. Bureau of Indian Affairs schools also attempt to meet the unique needs of handicapped Indian children in special education programs. These programs include classroom instruction, instruction in physical education, home instruction and other related services.

The Bureau of Indian Affairs budget process is unique in the federal budgeting system, in that it provides Indian tribes and Alaska natives with an opportunity to help shape the Bureau of Indian Affairs' request for funds by stating their priorities. It is important to note that priorities set by tribes in their portion of the budget process will not be changed by either the area or central office without consultation with the tribe. However, tribes may propose to reprogram funds when their priorities have changed following the actual appropriation. With the tribal priorities in hand, the central office in Washington develops a Bureau of Indian Affairs plan for the fiscal year.

With the possible exception of higher education scholarship funds and some employment assistance, urban Indians receive few services from the Bureau of Indian Affairs.

The scarcity of available jobs on Indian reservations has led many Indians to cities in search of work. In recent years, there also has been a movement of young Native Americans who received their education at colleges and universities back to their reservations. These Indians are dedicated to using the skills they have acquired to benefit their tribes, and many are assuming leadership roles within tribal governments.

*Above:* The annual Rocky Boy's Pow Wow near Box Elder, Montana. The Rocky Boy's Reservation is home to a band of Chippewa people whose name actually means "Stone Child," but which was mis-translated. The name stuck.

*Right:* A line-up of tepees for the annual Crow Fair. The event boasts the largest number of tepees at any single site anywhere in North America.

*Above right:* Hundreds of dancers participate in the annual Crow Fair.

# LOOKING TOWARD THE FUTURE

Indian reservations are affected by many of the same factors that affect the economies of other areas. Natural resources — timber, water, oil and gas, rich agricultural soil — can play a critical role in the development of economic growth. But there are other factors unique to Indian reservations. The trust status of the land, the sovereign immunity of the tribe, the tribal government and the way it operates, and other jurisdictional questions can have an effect on the success or failure of a tribal economy.

The role of tribal government is to create the climate for economic development. It is crucial that tribal government have stability and continuity. Only through stability and continuity can a tribe implement long-range plans. A tribe torn by internal factions that cannot work together or one that has an entirely new tribal government every two years will not have economic success.

The role of a tribal government in bringing about economic health usually is more difficult than its counterpart in a city or county off the reservation. A tribal government frequently is the developer, manager and operator of tribal enterprises, in addition to providing the normal governmental services within the boundaries of the reservation.

Tribal governments also have responsibility for attracting private investors and entrepreneurs to the reservations. Primarily, this means allaying the fears of potential investors of real or apparent risks stemming from unique conditions on the reservation. For example, if an investor is concerned about the lack of legal recourse in dealing with the tribe because of its sovereign immunity, the tribe might consider waiving its immunity. If businessmen are concerned they may have to go into tribal courts, the tribes must work to build confidence in the competence and impartiality of the tribal courts.

The trust status of Indian land is both a disadvantage and an advantage. The fact that it cannot be financially leveraged by mortgages or otherwise used as security for credit financing decreases the ability of Indian tribes and individuals to develop capital. On the other hand, tax exemptions, applying both to property taxes and income derived from trust resources, represents a significant advantage.

One distinction of a strong tribal government is its ability to influence tribal members to forego the immediate distribution of tribal funds so capital for tribal projects and programs can be accumulated.

Legislation governing judgment awards made by the Indian Claims Commission and the Court of Claims require tribes to use at least 20 percent for tribal programs and projects and to distribute no more than 80 percent to tribal members on a per capita basis. Some tribes have used judgment fund awards totally as a capital base for on-going tribal economic development, with no immediate per capita distribution.

*Right:* Hundreds of dancers celebrate Native American culture in the annual Red Earth Festival in Oklahoma.

The difficulties tribes encounter in seeking capital financing through conventional commercial routes are offset, in part, by federal programs administered by the Bureau of Indian Affairs which provide a revolving loan fund, a loan guaranty program, and an economic development "seed money" program.

The revolving loan fund program was inaugurated by the Indian Reorganization Act of 1934 and enlarged and solidified by the Indian Financing Act of 1974. The fund provides a source of financing for Indians who cannot borrow from other government credit agencies or from ordinary commercial lenders. Loans are made to tribes, Indian organizations and individual Indians for any purpose that will promote economic development on Indian reservations. Loans also are made to tribes and Indian organizations for relending to individual Indians and groups of Indians.

The loan guaranty program, which was initiated under the 1974 Indian Financing Act, provides access to private lenders through guaranteeing or insuring loans made to Indian tribes, organizations or individuals for economic development purposes. In addition to guaranteeing the loans, the program provides an interest subsidy which pays the difference between the private lender's interest rate and that charged by the Treasury for revolving fund loans.

*Above:* Seventeenth century life and culture is replicated at a recreated Powhatan Indian village near Jamestown, Virginia.

The Navajo tribe, whose reservation encompasses some 25,000 square miles in Arizona, New Mexico and Utah, has used the guaranteed loan program to help refinance its large Navajo Agricultural Products Industry. Loan guarantees have also helped Alaska native corporations established under provisions of the Alaska Native Claims Settlement Act. A direct loan of $550,000 enabled Native American steelworkers from the St. Regis Mohawk Tribe of New York to begin the American Mohawk Erectors and Riggers Corporation.

Meanwhile, the Jicarilla Apache tribe in New Mexico received a $500,000 grant to develop and operate a motel complex consisting of 40 guest rooms, a restaurant, a lounge and a gift shop on a five-acre site on the reservation.

*Above:* Recreating a seventeenth century canoe at the replica Indian village near Jamestown, Virginia calls for original methods. The log is hollowed out by literally burning out the interior.

The Makah tribe at Neah Bay, Washington, received a grant of $65,000 to purchase additional equipment for a sand and gravel enterprise. The Crow Creek tribe of South Dakota was given a grant of $187,500 toward a $750,000 project that will construct a maintenance building and grain storage facility to improve and expand its farm operations.

Other Bureau of Indian Affairs regular programs have had substantial effects on reservation economies. The protection of Indian rights and the real estate and financial trust services provided by the Bureau of Indian Affairs Office of Trust Responsibilities at least indirectly affect tribal economies — and sometimes have a dramatic and immediate impact when a tribe receives a large judgment award.

The Papago tribe in southern Arizona offers a good example of economic development through creative use of routine program funds. It used a tribal skill center and job training funds, together with some housing construction money, to build a successful tribal construction company. Starting with only three employees in April of 1982, the tribe combined training with work opportunities. The company moved from constructing individual housing units to building an $800,000 shopping center and a $3.3 million school. Several tribes own and operate their own major sawmill enterprises, including the Menominee in Wisconsin, the Red Lake Chippewa in Minnesota, the Navajo and

White Mountain Apache in Arizona, and the Confederated Tribes of the Warm Springs Reservation in Oregon.

The Menominee tribe has inhabited Northeast Wisconsin and Michigan's Upper Peninsula for generations, where ancestral tribal lands encompassed over 10 million acres. Following several treaties and land cessions, in 1854 the Menominee people were confined to their current reservation lands, totalling 235,000 acres. The Menominee Forest has survived as an island of timber in an ocean of cleared land. It is representative of the Lake States boreal forest that existed prior to clearing for farming by settlers. The tribe recognized that their future depended on the forest and embarked on a course of sustained yield management to avoid forest exploitation and preserve tribal existence. In order to survive off of this limited land base, the tribe decided that it must harvest timber, but must maintain and perpetuate the forest resources for future generations. The basic concept used was to harvest timber from one end of the reservation to the other in such a manner that when done, the first areas cut would be ready for cutting again.

The backbone to the tribal economy has been its forest product industry. The tribal enterprise has its origins back in 1908, when the sawmill was built in Neopit. Since the tribal forestry activities are not federally subsidized, the success of the sawmill depends on the steady flow of timber from forest to market. In the late 1990s, the enterprise employed approximately 125 people who are mostly tribal members, plus 180 additional woods workers.

The major cottage industry of the Native American community, arts and crafts, is only partially included in these minority business statistics. While they do include the Indian-owned shops that sell the products, they do not consider individual artists and craftsmen who produce the paintings, jewelry and other handicrafts.

In 1982, the Lac Courte Oreilles Band of Chippewa Indians in Wisconsin brought about a major turnaround of its tribal enterprises. It established a tribal business corporation and hired a professional business manager to direct the tribal enterprises. Over the next two decades, these enterprises would flourish, and the

*Above:* A young Florida Seminole woman in traditional costume. Recently, there has been a revival of Seminole culture in south Florida, an area from which the Seminole were evicted with great loss of life in the 1830s.

tribe would add radio station WOJB and the Lac Courte Oreilles Bingo Parlor and Casino. The Gila River Indian Community in Arizona is another tribe with a number of successful ventures. In addition to pioneering the development of a domestic rubber industry from the desert guayule shrub, the tribe has 63,000 acres of irrigated farm land, three industrial parks and a successful arts and crafts center. The Gila River tribe has been involved in research and development of the guayule shrub since 1975, and the United States Defense Department has entered into an agreement with the tribe for the cultivation of 5,000 acres of the shrub and construction of a processing facility. In 1983, the tribe signed an agreement with the Firestone Tire and Rubber Company to build a prototype plant on the reservation.

The Blackfeet tribe and about half of the 45 oil and gas producing tribes throughout the country have added energy departments to tribal administrative organizations. Many of these tribes have joined an organization called Council of Energy Resources Tribes (CERT), a nonprofit coalition of tribes that own energy resources. Founded in 1976, the organization initially was considered similar to an American Indian OPEC. In recent years, it has become less a political, lobbying organization and more a professional, technical assistance group. Earl Old Person, chief of the

*Below:* A pair of Seminole people dressed in traditional nineteenth century attire on Billie Swamp in the Florida Everglades. Compare this view to the pre-1921 photograph on page 178.

*Above:*  The Salish-Kootenai Community College is located at Pablo, Montana on the Flathead Reservation.

*Right:*  The Jocko River Trading Post in Ravalli, Montana dates back to the nineteenth century, when traders from Missoula came here to do business with the  people on the Flathead Reservation.

*Above right:*  The Confederated Salish and Kootenai Tribal Complex in Pablo, Montana is the administrative center for a reservation the size of the state of Delaware.

Blackfeet Indian tribe in Montana, made this statement in an article published by the Society of Exploration Geophysicists: "In the 1950s we sat silent and followed directions from oil companies. We followed orders from the Bureau of Indian Affairs. But in the 1960s our leaders began to speak up. Then in the 1970s we tried to find out how to profit from our resources other than getting more bonuses. Now, only recently, are we becoming knowledgeable and taking part in oil and gas operations."

Under a 1938 law, tribes were required to use standardized leasing procedures for the development of their minerals, but the Minerals Development Act of 1983 opened new possibilities by permitting joint ventures and other agreements in which the tribes maintained an active management role. The first contract approved by the Assistant Secretary under the new legislation was a joint venture agreement for the development of oil and gas on the Fort Peck Indian reservation in Montana. The contract between the Assiniboine and Dakota (Sioux) tribes of the reservation and the United States Energy Corporation called for the tribes and the company to share net proceeds from production on 1,360 acres after the company had paid the costs for drilling and bringing in the first producing well.

According to the Council of Energy Resources Tribes, tribal lands of CERT members contain approximately 50 percent of the country's privately owned uranium, 15 percent of the nation's total coal reserves, 30 percent of all Western low-sulfur strippable coal, four percent of all oil and natural gas reserves, and a substantial portion of the nation's oil-shale and geothermal reserves.

*The Indian Finance Digest*, published by the American Indian National Bank Scholarship Fund, recently noted that Indian tribes have four coal-producing mines ranked among the top 25 in the nation. The Kayenta Mine and the Navajo Mine — both located on the Navajo Reservation — are ranked 11th and 12th in production. The Black Mesa Mine on the Hopi reservation was eighteenth, and the Absaroka Mine on the Crow reservation, was twenty-third. As *The Wall Street Journal* pointed out in the 1980s, the Crow tribe, on its own, had become "the world's ninth-largest coal-owning country."

*Below:* A Cherokee potter at work in a demonstration at the Cherokee Reservation in North Carolina. There are seven times as many Cherokee people living in Oklahoma than in their traditional Carolina homeland.

*Above:* A Seminole woman in traditional garb in a replica nineteenth century village in Florida. Today, only a quarter of Seminoles still live in their traditional homeland of Florida. Most of the tribe lives in Oklahoma, to which the Seminole were "removed" in the 1830s.

In 1995, the United States Department of the Interior established a committee to advise the Minerals Management Service (MMS) on revising and simplifying regulations regarding valuation of natural gas produced on Native American lands. Designated as the Indian Gas Valuation Negotiated Rule Making Committee, it succeeds, by official transformation, an earlier, informal MMS study group which gathered information on the current gas market and identified challenges facing royalty valuation of gas from Indian leases.

The Committee had representatives from the Navajo Nation, the Jicarilla Apache tribe, the Native American Rights Fund, the Shoshone and Arapaho tribes of the Wind River Reservation, the Northern Ute, the Southern Ute tribe, the Council of Energy Resources Tribes, the Bureau of Indian Affairs, and the Minerals Management Service — all members of the earlier study group. New to the committee are representatives from industry, including Conoco and Meridian Oil.

Late in 1996, the Bureau of Indian Affairs announced that it had, under the Tribal Priority Allocation (TPA) program, distributed $140 million to priorities established by tribes and agencies. The Bureau of Indian Affairs' Aberdeen Area established a disaster team with the Sisseton-Wahpeton Sioux tribe for emergency response purposes such as ice storms, wherein seven portable generators were provided. At the Fort Totten Agency, the BIA worked in partnership with the Devils Lake Sioux tribe to get nearly $2 million in emergency relief for federally-owned facilities for the repair of flood-damaged roads. The partnership between the tribe and the agency allowed the tribe to relocate 43 homes and electrical utilities lines due to flooding.

# The New Century

After more than a century of defining Indian policy in the context of reservation and reserve programs, the governments of the United States and Canada have come full circle in their view of a government-to-government relationship with the tribes. At the beginning of the nineteenth century, tribes were conceived of as independent political entities. However, this view changed as the political entities with European roots became more powerful. Native Americans became an inconvenience, and were considered trespassers on land that was seen as belonging to white governments. Reservations were seen first as a place to confine a stateless people so that they wouldn't get in the way. Gradually, a view of Native Americans as wards of the state took hold, and the United States and Canada took on a paternal role.

Through much of the twentieth century, Native Americans, especially those living on reservations, sought to reassert their cultural identity. At the dawn of the twenty-first century, the tribes are seeking to reassert a tribal political identity, especially in the context of the reservations.

Tribal police and courts are taking on a greater role, especially in defining and enforcing the laws of particular reservations. Meanwhile, sovereignty is being reasserted in such venues as Indian gaming, a unique feature which has also provided economic benefits to tribes and reservations. The establishment of the vast Nunavut Territory in Canada is an exciting step in elevating the sovereign status of indigenous peoples in regions where they lived for centuries before the arrival of Europeans, and where they still represent a majority of the population.

The history of reservations and reserves in North America has been a long and not always pleasant story, but with the trends that are present today, the twenty-first century should hold an interesting and promising future for Native Americans.

*Above:* A Cherokee basketmaker at work. While basketry had an important role in traditional native cultures — especially in the East and in California — it is a popular craft for the modern tourist trade.

*Right:* A lone tepee on the Crow Reservation in Montana. As much as Native American culture has changed in the past two centuries, traditional cultural icons still play a role.

## APPENDIX I.

# RESERVATION POPULATION DATA: UNITED STATES

## ABERDEEN REGION

**Cheyenne River Agency**
Cheyenne River Reservation (SD) — 9,809

**Crow Creek Agency**
Crow Creek Reservation (SD) — 2,816

**Flandreau Santee Sioux**
Flandreau Reservation (SD) — 504

**Fort Berthold Agency**
Fort Berthold Reservation (ND) — 3,776

**Fort Totten Agency**
Fort Totten Reservation (ND) — 4,650

**Lower Brule Agency**
Lower Brule Reservation (SD) — 1,079

**Pine Ridge Agency**
Pine Ridge Reservation (SD) — 20,806

**Rosebud Agency**
Rosebud Reservation (SD) — 13,050

**Sisseton Agency**
Sisseton Reservation (SD) — 3,075

**Standing Rock Agency**
Standing Rock Reservation (ND) — 4,342
Standing Rock Reservation (SD) — 6,508

**Turtle Mountain Agency**
Trenton Field Office (MT) — 254
Trenton Field Office (ND) — 1,352
Turtle Mountain Reservation (ND) — 9,377

**Winnebago Agency**
Omaha Reservation (NE) — 5,227
Santee Sioux Reservation (NE) — 603
Winnebago Reservation (NE) — 1,204

**Yankton Agency**
Yankton Reservation (SD) — 4,053

ABERDEEN REGION Subtotal — 92,285

## ALBUQUERQUE REGION

**Jicarilla Agency**
Jicarilla Reservation (NM) — 3,353

**Laguna Agency**
Laguna Pueblo (NM) — 7,201

**Mescalero Reservation**
Mescalero Reservation (NM) — 4,289

**Northern Pueblo Agency**
Nambe Pueblo (NM) — 632
Picuris Pueblo (NM) — 236
Pojoaque Pueblo (NM) — 162
San Ildefonso Pueblo (NM) — 521
San Juan Pueblo (NM) — 2,246
Santa Clara Pueblo (NM) — 1,768
Taos Pueblo (NM) — 1,816
Tesuque Pueblo (NM) — 389

**Ramah-Navajo Agency** (NM) — 2,432

**Southern Pueblos Agency**
Acoma Pueblo (NM) — 6,091
Cochiti Pueblo (NM) — 1,037
Isleta Pueblo (NM) — 3,978
Jemez Pueblo (NM) — 3,030
San Felipe Pueblo (NM) — 2,938
Sandia Pueblo (NM) — 404
Santa Ana Pueblo (NM) — 639
Santo Domingo Pueblo (NM) — 3,860
Ysleta Del Sur (TX) — 1,284
Zia Pueblo (NM) — 849

**Southern Ute Agency**
Southern Ute Reservation (CO) — 2,254

**Ute Mountain Agency**
Ute Mountain Reservation (CO) — 1,325

**Zuni Agency**
Zuni Reservation (NM) — 8,725

ALBUQUERQUE REGION Subtotal — 61,439

## ANADARKO REGION

**Anadarko Agency**
Apache Tribe (OK) — 1,023
Caddo Tribe (OK) — 968
Comanche Tribe (OK) — 5,631
Delaware Tribe (OK) — 329
Fort Sill Apache Tribe (OK) — 111
Kiowa Tribe (OK) — 5,184
Wichita Tribe (OK) — 907

**Anadarko Area**
Alabama-Coushatta (TX) — 890

**Concho Agency**
Cheyenne-Arapaho Tribes (OK)                 7,543

**Horton Agency**
Iowa Tribe (KS)                                    377
Iowa Tribe (NE)                                     31
Kickapoo Tribe (KS)                                757
Prairie Band of Potawatomi (KS)                    781
Sac and Fox Iowa Tribe (NE)                          6
Sac and Fox of Missouri (KS)                        48

**Pawnee Agency**
Kaw Tribe (OK)                                     604
Otoe-Missouri Tribe (OK)                         1,412
Pawnee Tribe (OK)                                2,318
Ponca Tribe (OK)                                 2,581
Tonkawa Tribe (OK)                                 826

**Shawnee Agency**
Absentee-Shawnee (OK)                            1,180
Citizen Band Potawatomi Tribe (OK)               2,301
Iowa Tribe (OK)                                    555
Kickapoo Tribe (OK)                              1,336
Kickapoo Tribe (TX)                                450
Sac and Fox Tribe (OK)                           1,562

ANADARKO REGION Subtotal                        39,713

## BILLINGS REGION

**Blackfeet Agency**
Blackfeet Tribe (MT)                             7,782

**Crow Agency**
Crow Tribe (MT)                                  6,636

**Fort Belknap Agency**
Fort Belknap Reservation (MT)                    3,652

**Fort Peck Agency**
Fort Peck Tribes (MT)                            6,497

**Northern Cheyenne Agency**
Northern Cheyenne (MT)                           4,334

**Rocky Boy's Agency**
Rocky Boy's (MT)                                 2,992

**Wind River Agency**
Wind River Reservation (WY)                      8,038

BILLINGS REGION Subtotal                        39,931

## EASTERN REGION

**Area Field Offices**
Houlton Band of Maliseet (ME)                      560
Mashantucket Pequot Tribe (CT)                     155
Miccosukee Tribe (FL)                              550

Narragansett Tribe (RI)                          2,058
Passamaquoddy Tribe (ME)                           563
Penobscot Tribe (ME)                             1,051
Pleasant Point (ME)                                856

**Cherokee Agency**
Eastern Cherokee (NC)                           10,114

**Choctaw Agency**
Coushatta Tribe  (LA)                              362
Mississippi Choctaw Tribe (MS)                   5,438
Wampanoag Tribe (MA)                               646

**Eastern Area Office**
Chitimacha Tribe (LA)                              454
Poarch Creek Indians (AL)                        1,488
Tunica-Biloxi Tribe (LA)                           176

**New York Liaison Office**
Cayuga Nation (NY)                                 456
Oneida Nation (NV)                               1,109
Onondaga Nation (NY)                             1,034
Seneca Nation (NY)                               3,742
St. Regis Mohawk Tribe (NY)                      3,631
Tonawanda Band of Senecas (NY)                     689
Tuscarora Nation (NY)                              664

**Seminole Agency**
Seminole Tribe (FL)                              2,181

EASTERN REGION Subtotal                         37,709

## JUNEAU REGION

Anchorage Agency (AK)                           27,484
Bethel Agency (AK)                              18,762
Fairbanks Agency (AK)                           15,088
Nome Agency (AK)                                13,487
Southeast Agency (AK)                           87,644

JUNEAU REGION Subtotal                         162,465

## MINNEAPOLIS REGION

**Great Lakes Agency**
Bad River Reservation (WI)                       2,110
Forest County Potawatomi (WI)                      462
Lac Courte Oreilles (WI)                         4,037
Lac Du Flambeau Reservation (WI)                 1,274
Oneida Reservation (WI)                          5,649
Red Cliff Reservation (WI)                       1,651
St. Croix Reservation (WI)                       1,409
Sokagoan Chippewa Tribe (WI)                       512

Stockbridge-Munsee Tribe (WI)                      936
Wisconsin-Winnebago Tribe (WI)                   2,608

**Menominee Field Office**
Menominee Reservation (WI)                       5,422

**Michigan Agency**
Bay Mills Reservation (MI)                     637
Grand Traverse Band (MI)                     2,363
Hannahville Community (MI)                     347
Isabella Reservation (MI)                      758
Keweenaw-L'Anse Reservation (MI)              910
La Vieux Desert (MI)                           185
Sault Ste. Marie Tribe (MI)                 10,134

**Minnesota Agency (North)**
Fond Du Lac Reservation (MN)                3,265
Grand Portage Reservation (MN)                349
Leech Lake Reservation (MN)                 5,803
Mille Lacs Reservation (MN)                 1,369
Nett Lake Reservation (MN)                  2,015
White Earth Reservation (MN)                4,480

**Minnesota Agency (South)**
Lower Sioux Reservation (MN)                  388
Prairie Island Reservation (MN)               176
Shakopee Sioux Reservation (MN)               230
Upper Sioux Reservation (MN)                  304

**Red Lake Agency**
Red Lake Reservation (MN)                   5,126

**Sac and Fox Field Office**
Sac and Fox Tribe (IA)                        886

MINNEAPOLIS REGION Subtotal               65,805


## MUSKOGEE REGION

**Ardmore Agency**
Chickasaw (OK)                             13,695

**Miami Agency**
Eastern Shawnee Tribe (OK)                    429
Miami Tribe (OK)                              836
Modoc Tribe (OK)                              218
Ottawa Tribe (OK)                             684
Peoria Tribe (OK)                           1,181
Quapaw Tribe (OK)                           2,348
Seneca-Cayuga (OK)                            788
Wyandotte (OK)                              2,203

**Okmulgee Agency**
Muskogee (Creek) Nation (OK)               76,251

**Osage Agency**
Osage Tribe (OK)                           10,594

**Tahlequah Agency**
Cherokee Nation (OK)                       75,940

**Talihina Agency**
Choctaw Nation (OK)                        44,717

**Wewoka Agency**
Seminole Nation (OK)                        6,536

MUSKOGEE REGION Subtotal                  236,197

## NAVAJO REGION

Chinle Agency (AZ)                         28,290

**Eastern Navajo Agency**
Eastern Navajo (NM)                        41,820

**Fort Defiance Agency**
Fort Defiance (AZ)                         38,397
Fort Defiance (NM)                         12,321

**Shiprock Agency**
**Shiprock (AZ)**                           9,335
Shiprock (NM)                              39,467
Shiprock (UT)                               3,827

**Western Navajo Agency**
Western Navajo (AZ)                        32,619
Western Navajo (UT)                         3,227

NAVAJO REGION Subtotal                    207,303

## PHOENIX REGION

**Colorado River Agency**
Chemehuevi Reservation (CA)                   132
Colorado River Reservation (CA)                51
Colorado River Tribes (AZ)                  1,665
Fort Mohave Tribe (AZ)                        421
Fort Mohave Tribe (CA)                        310

**Eastern Nevada Agency**
Duck Valley Reservation (ID)                  276
Duck Valley Reservation (NV)                1,002
Duckwater Shoshone (NV)                       118
Ely Colony (NV)                               279
Goshute Reservation (NV)                       22
Goshute Reservation (UT)                       78
Te Moak Band, Battle Mountain (NV)            674
Te Moak Band, Ely Colony (NV)               1,158
Te Moak Band, South Fork (NV)                 239
Te Moak Band, Wells Colony (NV)               144

**Fort Apache Agency**
Fort Apache Reservation (AZ)               13,575

**Fort Yuma Agency**
Cocopah Reservation (AZ)                      448

Quechan Reservation (CA)                    3,019

**Hopi Agency**
Hopi Reservation (AZ)                       9,583

**Papago Agency**
Tohono O'Odham Nation (AZ)                 18,900

**Pima Agency**
| | |
|---|---|
| Ak Chin Reservation (AZ) | 650 |
| Gila River Reservation (AZ) | 11,500 |

**Salt River Agency**
| | |
|---|---|
| Fort McDowell Reservation (AZ) | 887 |
| Pascua Yaqui Tribe (AZ) | 8,206 |
| Salt River Reservation (AZ) | 5,480 |

**San Carlos Agency**
| | |
|---|---|
| San Carlos Reservation (AZ) | 8,266 |

**Southern Paiute Field Station**
| | |
|---|---|
| Kaibab Reservation (AZ) | 113 |
| Las Vegas Colony (NV) | 114 |
| Moapa Reservation (NV) | 257 |
| Paiute Tribe (UT) | 850 |

**Truxton Canyon Agency**
| | |
|---|---|
| Camp Verde Reservation (AZ) | 800 |
| Havasupai Reservation (AZ) | 823 |
| Hualapai Reservation (AZ) | 1,800 |
| Payson Tonto Apache (AZ) | 145 |
| Yavapai Prescott Reservation (AZ) | 142 |

**Uintah and Ouray Agency**
| | |
|---|---|
| Skull Valley Reservation (AZ) | 91 |
| Uintah and Ouray Reservation (UT) | 3,205 |

**Western Nevada Agency**
| | |
|---|---|
| Fallon Colony and Reservation (NV) | 904 |
| Fort McDermitt Reservation (NV) | 621 |
| Lovelock Colony (NV) | 112 |
| Pyramid Lake Reservation (NV) | 1,603 |
| Reno-Sparks Colony (NV) | 850 |
| Stewart Community (NV) | 88 |
| Summit Lake Reservation (NV) | 13 |
| Walker River Reservation (NV) | 941 |
| Washoe Tribe, Carson Colony (NV) | 275 |
| Washoe Tribe, Dresslerville (NV) | 348 |
| Washoe Tribe, Woodfords (CA) | 299 |
| Winnemucca Colony (NV) | 61 |
| Yerington Colony (NV) | 337 |
| Yomba Reservation (NV) | 100 |

| | |
|---|---|
| PHOENIX REGION Subtotal | 101,386 |

## PORTLAND REGION

**Colville Agency**
| | |
|---|---|
| Colville Reservation (WA) | 4,633 |

**Flathead Agency**
| | |
|---|---|
| Salish and Kootenai Tribes (MT) | 7,667 |

**Fort Hall Agency**
| | |
|---|---|
| Fort Hall Reservation (ID) | 6,877 |
| NW Band of Shoshone Nation (UT) | 411 |

**Metlakatla Field Office**
| | |
|---|---|
| Annette Island Reservation (AK) | 1,412 |

**Northern Idaho Agency**
| | |
|---|---|
| Coeur D'Alene Reservation (ID) | 803 |
| Kootenai Tribe (ID) | 143 |
| Nez Perce Reservation (ID) | 1,834 |

**Olympic Peninsula Agency**
| | |
|---|---|
| Chehalis Reservation (WA) | 775 |
| Hoh Reservation (WA) | 85 |
| Jamestown Klallam Tribe (WA) | 416 |
| Lower Elwha Klallam Tribe (WA) | 1,149 |
| Makah Reservation (WA) | 1,752 |
| Quileute Reservation (WA) | 784 |
| Quinault Reservation (WA) | 2,951 |
| Shoalwater Reservation (WA) | 371 |
| Skokomish Reservation (WA) | 1,223 |
| Squaxin Island Reservation (WA) | 1,539 |

**Puget Sound Agency**
| | |
|---|---|
| Lummi Reservation (WA) | 4,200 |
| Muckleshoot Reservation (WA) | 3,144 |
| Nisqually Reservation (WA) | 2,498 |
| Nooksack Tribe (WA) | 740 |
| Port Gamble Reservation (WA) | 676 |
| Puyallup Reservation (WA) | 12,312 |
| Sauk-Suiattle Reservation (WA) | 273 |
| Stillaquamish Reservation (WA) | 512 |
| Suquamish Tribal Council (WA) | 953 |
| Swinomish Reservation (WA) | 935 |
| Tulalip Reservation (WA) | 3,889 |
| Upper Skagit Tribe (WA) | 457 |

**Siletz Agency**
| | |
|---|---|
| Coos Bay Tribes (OR) | 286 |
| Coquille Tribe (OR) | 387 |
| Cow Creek Tribes (OR) | 436 |
| Grand Ronde Tribes (OR) | 3,580 |
| Siletz Reservation (OR) | 1,789 |

**Spokane Agency**
| | |
|---|---|
| Kalispel Reservation (WA) | 186 |
| Spokane Reservation (WA) | 1,230 |

**Umatilla Agency**
| | |
|---|---|
| Umatilla Reservation (OR) | 1,850 |

**Warm Springs Agency**
| | |
|---|---|
| Burns-Paiute Colony (OR) | 219 |
| Confederated Tribes of Warm Springs (OR) | 2,533 |
| Klamath Tribe (OR) | 2,515 |

**Yakima Agency**
| | |
|---|---|
| Yakima Reservation (WA) | 13,741 |

| | |
|---|---|
| PORTLAND REGION Subtotal | 94,166 |

## SACRAMENTO REGION

### Central California

| | |
|---|---:|
| Benton Paiute Reservation (CA) | 48 |
| Berry Creek Rancheria (CA) | 304 |
| Big Pine Rancheria (CA) | 367 |
| Big Sandy Rancheria (CA) | 188 |
| Big Valley Rancheria (CA) | 211 |
| Bishop Reservation (CA) | 1,350 |
| Bridgeport Colony (CA) | 55 |
| Buena Vista Rancheria (CA) | 1 |
| Chicken Ranch Rancheria (CA) | 10 |
| Chico Rancheria (CA) | 45 |
| Cloverdale Rancheria (CA) | 273 |
| Cold Springs Rancheria (CA) | 265 |
| Colusa Rancheria (CA) | 71 |
| Cortina Rancheria (CA) | 150 |
| Coyota Valley Band (CA) | 274 |
| Dry Creek Rancheria (CA) | 163 |
| Enterprise Rancheria (CA) | 177 |
| Fort Independence Reservation (CA) | 123 |
| Greenville Rancheria (CA) | 317 |
| Grindstone Rancheria (CA) | 171 |
| Guidiville Reservation (CA) | 115 |
| Hopland Rancheria (CA) | 353 |
| Jackson Rancheria (CA) | 27 |
| Laytonville Rancheria (CA) | 504 |
| Lone Pine Reservation (CA) | 296 |
| Lytton Reservation (CA) | 183 |
| Manchester Point Arena Rancheria (CA) | 253 |
| Middletown Rancheria (CA) | 95 |
| Mooretown Rancheria (CA) | 808 |
| North Fork Rancheria (CA) | 280 |
| Picayune Rancheria (CA) | 769 |
| Pinoleville Rancheria (CA) | 161 |
| Potter Valley Rancheria (CA) | 187 |
| Redwood Valley Rancheria (CA) | 129 |
| Robinson Rancheria (CA) | 211 |
| Round Valley Rancheria (CA) | 1,131 |
| Rumsey Rancheria (CA) | 51 |
| Santa Rosa Rancheria (CA) | 356 |
| Scotts Valley (Pomo) (CA) | 147 |
| Sherwood Valley Rancheria (CA) | 274 |
| Shingle Springs Rancheria (CA) | 185 |
| Stewarts Point Rancheria (CA) | 248 |
| Sulphur Bank Rancheria (CA) | 221 |
| Table Mountain Rancheria (CA) | 115 |
| Timbi-Sha Reservation (CA) | 209 |
| Tule River Reservation (CA) | 957 |
| Tuolumne Rancheria (CA) | 288 |
| Upper Lake Rancheria (CA) | 188 |

### Northern California Agency

| | |
|---|---:|
| Alturas Rancheria (CA) | 153 |
| Big Lagoon Rancheria (CA) | 24 |
| Blue Lake Rancheria (CA) | 33 |
| Cedarville Rancheria (CA) | 25 |
| Elk Valley Rancheria (CA) | 188 |
| Fort Bidwell Reservation (CA) | 177 |
| Hoopa Valley (CA) | 2,393 |
| Karuk Reservation (CA) | 5,100 |
| Pit River Tribe (CA) | 2,329 |
| Quartz Valley Rancheria (CA) | 264 |
| Redding Rancheria (CA) | 6,589 |
| Resighini Rancheria (CA) | 85 |
| Rohnerville Rancheria (CA) | 298 |
| Smith River Rancheria (CA) | 387 |
| Susanville Rancheria (CA) | 538 |
| Table Bluff Rancheria (CA) | 239 |
| Trinidad Rancheria (CA) | 128 |
| Yurok Reservation (CA) | 3,450 |

### Palm Springs Field Station

| | |
|---|---:|
| Agua Caliente Reservation (CA) | 286 |

### Southern California Agency

| | |
|---|---:|
| Augustine Reservation (CA) | 8 |
| Barona Reservation (CA) | 420 |
| Cabazon Reservation (CA) | 28 |
| Cahuilla Reservation (CA) | 217 |
| Campo Reservation (CA) | 184 |
| Capitan Grande Reservation (CA) | 36 |
| Cuyapaipe Reservation (CA) | 17 |
| Inaja and Cosmit Reservation (CA) | 17 |
| Jamul Village (CA) | 60 |
| La Jolla Reservation (CA) | 401 |
| La Posta Reservation (CA) | 9 |
| Los Coyotes Reservation (CA) | 254 |
| Manzanita Reservation (CA) | 81 |
| Mesa Grande Reservation (CA) | 70 |
| Morongo Reservation (CA) | 1,147 |
| Pala Reservation (CA) | 838 |
| Pauma Reservation (CA) | 119 |
| Pechanga Reservation (CA) | 725 |
| Ramona Band (CA) | 3 |
| Rincon Reservation (CA) | 432 |
| San Manuel Reservation (CA) | 80 |
| San Pasqual Reservation (CA) | 1,698 |
| Santa Rosa Reservation (CA) | 135 |
| Santa Ynez Reservation (CA) | 312 |
| San Ysabel Reservation (CA) | 953 |
| Soboba Reservation (CA) | 725 |
| Sycuan Reservation (CA) | 120 |
| Torres-Martinez Reservation (CA) | 260 |
| Twentynine Palms Reservation (CA) | 14 |
| Viejas Reservation (CA) | 213 |
| | |
| SACRAMENTO REGION Subtotals | 45,568 |

## UNITED STATES TOTAL    1,183,967

# APPENDIX II.

# RESERVE AND NON-RESERVE POPULATION DATA: CANADA

*Note: The first figure given is the total affiliated population. The second figure is that residing upon the reserve.*

## ATLANTIC REGION

**Atlantic Regional Office District**
District Subtotal (1,883)                          1,111

**New Brunswick District**
District Subtotal (9,313)                          6,183

**Nova Scotia District**
District Subtotal (9,787)                          6,594

ATLANTIC REGION
Subtotal (20,983)                                 13,888

## QUEBEC REGION

**Quebec District**
Nation Huronne (Huron) Wendat (2,603)                 66
Other (12,227)                                     9006
District Subtotal (14,830)                         9,972

**L'Abitibi Algonquin District**
Long Point First Nations (520)                        0
Cree Nation of Chisasibi (2,614)                   2,442
Cree Nation of Wemindji (1,035)                      904
Other (6,758)                                      5,671
District Subtotal (10,927)                         9,017

**Montreal District**
Mohawks of Kahnawake (7,743)                       6,438
Abenakis de Wolinak (305)                             84
Other (5,144)                                      2,667
District Subtotal (13,192)                         9,189

QUEBEC REGION Subtotal (51,754)                   35,354

## ONTARIO REGION

**Sudbury District**
Batchewana First Nation (1,577)                      570
Chapleau Cree First Nation(234)                       24
Other (20,596)                                     8,753
District Subtotal (22,407)                         9,347

**Southern Brantford District**
Six Nations of the Grand River (0)                    0
Wasauksing First Nation (800)                        272
Chippewas of Rama First Nation (989)                 426

Mohawks of Akwesasne (7,591)                       5,208
Curve Lake First Nation (1,416)                      782
Hiawatha First Nation (369)                          161
Mohawks of the Bay of Quinte (5,570)               1,871
Chippewas of the Thames
    First Nation (1,760)           685
Chippewas of Kettle Point,
    Stony Point and Sarnia (3,045)  1,328
Tuscarora (1,562)                                    706
Oneida (1,455)                                       590
Onondaga Clear Sky and
    Bearfoot Onondaga (933)          508
Upper and Lower Cayuga (2,546)                     2,342
Konadaha and Niharondasa Seneca (654)                254
Lower, Walker and Upper Mohawk (7,098)             3,572
Other (25,135)                                    10,657
District Subtotal (60,923)                        29,362

**Bruce Southampton District**
Chippewas of Nawash (1,699)                          642
Other (1,225)                                        654
District Subtotal (2,924)                          1,296

**Western District**
Grassy Narrows First Nation (902)                    573
Wabigoon Lake Ojibway Nation (326)                   119
Eabametoong First Nation (1,597)                     845
Ginoogaming First Nation (530)                       200
Ojibway of the Pic River
    First Nation (769)              402
Other (17,937)                                     7,544
District Subtotal (22,061)                         9,683

**Sioux Lookout District**
District Subtotal (13,006)                         9,774

ONTARIO REGION
Subtotal (121,321)                                59,462

## MANITOBA REGION

**Manitoba Regional Office District**
Brokenhead Ojibway Nation Band (1,097)               322
Buffalo Point First Nation (72)                       33
Cross Lake (4,247)                                 3,091
Poplar River First Nation (931)                      842
Waywayseecappo First Nation
    Treaty Four (1,432)              933
Grand Rapids First Nation (865)                      444
Opaskwayak Cree Nation (2,922)                     2,030
Other (57,493)                                    35,975
District Subtotal (69,059)                        43,670

**Thompson District**

| | |
|---|---:|
| Sayisi Dene First Nation (564) | 268 |
| Shamattawa First Nation (860) | 787 |
| Other (9,988) | 5,830 |
| District Subtotal (11,412) | 6,885 |

| | |
|---|---:|
| MANITOBA REGION Subtotal (80,471) | 50,555 |

## SASKATCHEWAN REGION

**North Battleford District**

| | |
|---|---:|
| District Subtotal (11,423) | 5,371 |

**Prince Albert District**

| | |
|---|---:|
| Shoal Lake Band of the Cree Nation (528) | 422 |
| Other (21,242) | 13,232 |
| District Subtotal (21,770) | 13,654 |

**Yorkton District**

| | |
|---|---:|
| District Subtotal (11,290) | 3,477 |

**Saskatoon District**

| | |
|---|---:|
| District Subtotal (9,309) | 3,690 |

**Touchwood-File Hills
    Qu'appelle District**

| | |
|---|---:|
| District Subtotal (16,877) | 6,588 |

**Meadow Lake District**

| | |
|---|---:|
| District Subtotal (8,081) | 4,201 |

**Shellbrook District**

| | |
|---|---:|
| District Subtotal (5,080) | 3,122 |

| | |
|---|---:|
| SASKATCHEWAN REGION Subtotal (83,830) | 44,103 |

## NORTHWEST TERRITORIES REGION

**Northwest Territories
    Regional Office District**

| | |
|---|---:|
| District Subtotal (11,805) | 202 |

| | |
|---|---:|
| NORTHWEST TERRITORIES REGION Subtotal (11,805) | 202 |

## YUKON REGION

**Yukon Regional Office District**

| | |
|---|---:|
| Kwanlin Dun First Nation (1,118) | 25 |
| Kluane First Nation (137) | N/A |
| Other (4,599) | 326 |
| District Subtotal (5,854) | 351 |

| | |
|---|---:|
| YUKON REGION Subtotal (5,854) | 351 |

## ALBERTA REGION

**Alberta Regional Office District**

| | |
|---|---:|
| Bigstone Cree Nation (4,003) | 1,479 |
| Mikisew Cree First Nation (1,658) | 1 |
| Other (21,167) | 12,426 |
| District Subtotal (26,828) | 13,906 |

**Southern Alberta District**

| | |
|---|---:|
| Siksika Nation (4,298) | 2,486 |
| Tsuu T'ina Nation (1,099) | 835 |
| Sunchild First Nation (644) | 322 |
| Blood (7,592) | 6,059 |
| Peigan (2,652) | 1,735 |
| Other (1,571) | 1,387 |
| District Subtotal (17,856) | 12,824 |

**St. Paul District**

| | |
|---|---:|
| Saddle Lake (6,263) | 4,497 |
| Other (5,055) | 2,784 |
| District Subtotal (11,318) | 7,281 |

**Fort McMurray District**

| | |
|---|---:|
| District Subtotal (4,372) | 551 |

**Fort Vermillion District**

| | |
|---|---:|
| Beaver First Nation (580) | 283 |
| Little Red River Cree Nation (2,328) | 1,685 |
| Other (2,613) | 1,734 |
| District Subtotal (5,521) | 3,702 |

| | |
|---|---:|
| ALBERTA REGION Subtotal (65,895) | 38,264 |

## BRITISH COLUMBIA REGION

**Hazelton District**

| | |
|---|---:|
| District Subtotal (7,024) | 3,187 |

**Vancouver Island District**

| | |
|---|---:|
| District Subtotal (14,531) | 7,911 |

**Campbell River District**

| | |
|---|---:|
| District Subtotal (5,502) | 2,341 |

**Central Vancouver District**

| | |
|---|---:|
| District Subtotal (13,875) | 7,247 |

**Prince George District**

| | |
|---|---:|
| Lheit Lit'en Nation (212) | 34 |
| Tl'azt'en Nations (1,272) | 895 |
| Cheslatta Carrier Nation (210) | 85 |
| Other (8,886) | 4,328 |
| District Subtotal (10,580) | 5,342 |

**Northwest District**

| | |
|---|---:|
| Lax Kw'alaams (2,322) | 1,021 |
| Gitlakdamix (1,417) | 666 |
| Other (13,148) | 4,593 |
| District Subtotal (16,887) | 6,280 |

**Vancouver District**
Nuxalk Nation (1,102)                      694
Other (16,412)                           8,927
District Subtotal (17,514)               9,621

**Williams Lake District**
District Subtotal (5,363)                3,406

BRITISH COLUMBIA REGION
Subtotal (91,276)                       45,335

**CANADA TOTAL (533,189)        283,514**

# APPENDIX III.

# FEDERALLY-RECOGNIZED US TRIBES AND NATIONS

Absentee-Shawnee Tribe of Indians of Oklahoma

Agua Caliente Band of Cahuilla Indians of the Agua Caliente Reservation, California

Ak Chin Community of Papago Indians of the Maricopa, Ak Chin Reservation, Arizona

Alabama and Coushatta Tribes of Texas

Alabama-Quassarte Tribal Town of the Creek Nation of Oklahoma

Alturas Rancheria of Pit River Indians of California

Apache Tribe of Oklahoma

Arapaho Tribe of the Wind River Reservation, Wyoming

Aroostook Band of Micmac Indians of Maine

Assiniboine and Sioux Tribes of the Fort Peck Reservation, Montana

Augustine Band of Cahuilla Mission Indians of the Augustine Reservation, California

Bad River Band of the Lake Superior Tribe of Chippewa Indians of the Bad River Reservation,   Wisconsin

Barona Group of Capitan Grande Band of Mission Indians of the Barona Reservation, California

Bay Mills Community of the Sault Ste. Marie Band of Chippewa Indians, Bay Mills Reservation, Michigan

Bear River Band of the Rohnerville Rancheria of California

Berry Creek Rancheria of Maidu Indians of California

Big Lagoon Rancheria of Smith River Indians of California

Big Pine Band of Owens Valley Paiute Shoshone Indians of the Big Pine Reservation, California

Big Sandy Rancheria of Mono Indians of California

Big Valley Rancheria of Pomo and Pit River Indians of California

Blackfeet Tribe of the Blackfeet Reservation of Montana

Blue Lake Rancheria of California

Bridgeport Paiute Colony of California

Buena Vista Rancheria of Me-Wuk (Miwok) Indians of California

Burns Paiute Tribe of the Burns Paiute Colony of Oregon

Cabazon Band of Cahuilla Mission Indians of the Cabazon Reservation, California

Cachil DeHe Band of Wintun Indians of the Colusa Community of the Colusa Rancheria, California

Caddo Tribe of Oklahoma

Cahuilla Band of Mission Indians of the Cahuilla Reservation, California

Cahto Tribe of the Laytonville Rancheria, California

Campo Band of Diegueno Mission Indians of the Campo Reservation, California

Capitan Grande Band of Diegueno Mission Indians of California

Catawba Tribe of South Carolina

Cayuga Nation of New York

Cedarville Rancheria of Northern Paiute Indians of California

Chemehuevi Tribe of the Chemehuevi Reservation, California

Cher-Ae Heights Community of the Trinidad Rancheria, California

Cherokee Nation of Oklahoma

Cheyenne-Arapaho Tribes of Oklahoma

Cheyenne River Sioux Tribe of the Cheyenne River Reservation, South Dakota

Chickasaw Nation of Oklahoma

Chicken Ranch Rancheria of Me-Wuk (Miwok) Indians of California

Chippewa-Cree Indians of the Rocky Boy's Reservation, Montana

Chitimacha Tribe of Louisiana

Choctaw Nation of Oklahoma

Citizen Band Potawatomi Tribe of Oklahoma

Cloverdale Rancheria of Pomo Indians of California

Coast Community of Yurok Indians of the Resighini Rancheria, California

Cocopah Tribe of Arizona

Coeur D'Alene Tribe of the Coeur D'Alene Reservation, Idaho

Cold Springs Rancheria of Mono Indians of California

Colorado River Tribes of the Colorado River Reservation, Arizona and California

Comanche Tribe of Oklahoma

Confederated Salish and Kootenai Tribes of the Flathead Reservation, Montana

Confederated Tribes of the Chehalis Reservation, Washington

Confederated Tribes of the Colville Reservation, Washington

Confederated Tribes of the Coos, Lower Umpqua and Siuslaw Indians of Oregon

Confederated Tribes of the Goshute Reservation, Nevada and Utah

Confederated Tribes of the Grand Ronde Community of Oregon

Confederated Tribes of the Siletz Reservation, Oregon

Confederated Tribes of the Umatilla Reservation, Oregon

Confederated Tribes of the Warm Springs Reservation of Oregon

Confederated Tribes and Bands of the Yakima Nation of the Yakima Reservation, Washington

Coquille Tribe of Oregon

Cortina Rancheria of Wintun Indians of California

Coushatta Tribe of Louisiana

Cow Creek Band of Umpqua Indians of Oregon

Coyote Valley Band of Pomo Indians of California

Crow Creek Sioux Tribe of the Crow Creek Reservation, South Dakota

Crow Tribe of Montana

Cuyapaipe Community of Diegueno Mission Indians of the Cuyapaipe Reservation, California

Death Valley Timbi-Sha Shoshone Band of California

Delaware Tribe of Western Oklahoma

Devils Lake Sioux Tribe of the Devils Lake Sioux Reservation, North Dakota

Dry Creek Rancheria of Pomo Indians of California

Duckwater Shoshone Tribe of the Duckwater Reservation, Nevada

Eastern Band of Cherokee Indians of North Carolina

Eastern Shawnee Tribe of Oklahoma

Elem Colony of Pomo Indians of the Sulphur Bank Rancheria, California

Elk Valley Rancheria of California

Ely Shoshone Tribe of Nevada

Enterprise Rancheria of Maidu Indians of California

Flandreau Santee Sioux Tribe of South Dakota

Forest County Potawatomi Community of Wisconsin Potawatomi Indians, Wisconsin

Fort Belknap Community of the Fort Belknap Reservation of Montana

Fort Bidwell Community of Paiute Indians of the Fort Bidwell Reservation, California

Fort Independence Community of Paiute Indians of the Fort Independence Reservation, California

Fort McDermitt Paiute and Shoshone Tribes of the Fort McDermitt Reservation, Nevada

Fort McDowell Mohave-Apache Community of the Fort McDowell Reservation, Arizona

Fort Mohave Tribe of Arizona

Fort Sill Apache Tribe of Oklahoma

Gila River Pima-Maricopa Community of the Gila River Reservation of Arizona

Grand Traverse Band of Ottawa and Chippewa Indians of Michigan

Greenville Rancheria of Maidu Indians of California

Grindstone Rancheria of Wintun-Wailaki Indians of California

Guidiville Rancheria of California

Hannahville Community of Wisconsin Potawatomi Indians of Michigan

Havasupai Tribe of the Havasupai Reservation, Arizona

Ho-Chunk Nation of Wisconsin (formerly known as the Wisconsin Winnebago Tribe)

Hoh Tribe of the Hoh Reservation, Washington

Hoopa Valley Tribe of the Hoopa Valley Reservation, California

Hopi Tribe of Arizona

Hopland Band of Pomo Indians of the Hopland Reservation, California

Houlton Band of Maliseet Indians of Maine

Hualapai Tribe of the Hualapai Reservation, Arizona

Inaja Band of Diegueno Mission Indians of the Inaja and Cosmit Reservation, California

Ione Band of Miwok Indians of California

Iowa Tribe of Kansas and Nebraska

Iowa Tribe of Oklahoma

Jackson Rancheria of Me-Wuk (Miwok) Indians of California

Jamestown Klallam Tribe of Washington

Jamul Village of California

Jicarilla Apache Tribe of the Jicarilla Apache Reservation, New Mexico

Kaibab Band of Paiute Indians of the Kaibab Reservation, Arizona

Kalispel Community of the Kalispel Reservation, Washington

Karuk Tribe of California

Kashia Band of Pomo Indians of the Stewarts Point Rancheria, California

Kaw Tribe of Oklahoma

Keweenaw Bay Community of L'Anse and Ontonagon Bands of Chippewa Indians of the L'Anse Reservation, Michigan

Kickapoo Traditional Tribe of Texas

Kialegee Tribal Town of the Creek Nation of Oklahoma

Kickapoo Tribe of Indians of the Kickapoo Reservation in Kansas

Kickapoo Tribe of Oklahoma

Kiowa Tribe of Oklahoma

Klamath Tribe of Oregon

Kootenai Tribe of Idaho

La Jolla Band of Luiseno Mission Indians of the
La Jolla Reservation, California

La Posta Band of Diegueno Mission Indians of the
La Posta Reservation, California

Lac Courte Oreilles Band of Lake Superior Chippewa
Indians of the Lac Courte Oreilles Reservation
of Wisconsin

Lac du Flambeau Band of Lake Superior Chippewa
Indians of the Lac du Flambeau Reservation of
Wisconsin

Lac Vieux Desert Band of Lake Superior Chippewa
Indians of Michigan

Las Vegas Tribe of Paiute Indians of the Las Vegas
Colony, Nevada

Little River Band of Ottawa Indians of Michigan Little
Traverse Bay Bands of Ottawa Indians of
Michigan

Los Coyotes Band of Cahuilla Mission Indians of the
Los Coyotes Reservation, California

Lovelock Paiute Tribe of the Lovelock Colony,
Nevada

Lower Brule Sioux Tribe of the Lower Brule
Reservation, South Dakota

Lower Elwha Tribal Community of the Lower Elwha
Reservation, Washington

Lower Sioux Community of Minnesota
Mdewakanton Sioux Indians of the Lower
Sioux Reservation in Minnesota

Lummi Tribe of the Lummi Reservation, Washington

Lytton Reservation of California

Makah Tribe of the Makah Reservation, Washington

Manchester Band of Pomo Indians of the
Manchester-Point Arena Rancheria, California

Manzanita Band of Diegueno Mission Indians of the
Manzanita Reservation, California

Mashantucket Pequot Tribe of Connecticut

Mechoopda Tribe of Chico Rancheria, California

Menominee Tribe of Wisconsin

Mesa Grande Band of Diegueno Mission Indians of the
Mesa Grande Reservation, California

Mescalero Apache Tribe of the Mescalero Reservation,
New Mexico

Miami Tribe of Oklahoma

Miccosukee Tribe of Indians of Florida

Middletown Rancheria of Pomo Indians of California

Minnesota Chippewa Tribe, Minnesota
    Bois Forte Band (Nett Lake)
    Fond du Lac Band
    Grand Portage Band
    Leech Lake Band
    Mille Lac Band
    White Earth Band

Mississippi Band of Choctaw Indians, Mississippi

Moapa Band of Paiute Indians of the Moapa River
Reservation, Nevada

Modoc Tribe of Oklahoma

Mohegan Tribe of Connecticut

Mooretown Rancheria of Maidu Indians of California

Morongo Band of Cahuilla Mission Indians of the
Morongo Reservation, California

Muckleshoot Tribe of the Muckleshoot
Reservation, Washington

Muskogee (Creek) Nation of Oklahoma

Narragansett Tribe of Rhode Island

Navajo Tribe of Arizona, New Mexico and Utah

Nez Perce Tribe of Idaho

Nisqually Tribe of the Nisqually Reservation,
Washington

Nooksack Tribe of Washington

Northern Cheyenne Tribe of the Northern Cheyenne Reservation, Montana

Northfork Rancheria of Mono Indians of California

Northwestern Band of the Shoshone Nation of Utah (Washakie)

Oglala Sioux Tribe of the Pine Ridge Reservation, South Dakota

Omaha Tribe of Nebraska

Oneida Nation

Oneida Tribe of Wisconsin

Onondaga Nation of New York

Osage Nation of Oklahoma

Otoe-Missouri Tribe of Oklahoma

Ottawa Tribe of Oklahoma

Paiute Tribe of Utah

Paiute-Shoshone Indians of the Bishop Community of the Bishop Colony, California

Paiute-Shoshone Tribe of the Fallon Reservation and Colony, Nevada

Paiute-Shoshone Tribe of the Lone Pine Community of the Lone Pine Reservation, California

Pala Band of Luiseno Mission Indians of the Pala Reservation, California

Pascua Yaqui Tribe of Arizona

Paskenta Band of Nomlaki Indians of California

Passamaquoddy Tribe of Maine

Pauma Band of Luiseno Mission Indians of the Pauma and Yuma Reservation, California

Pawnee Tribe of Oklahoma

Pechanga Band of Luiseno Mission Indians of the Pechanga Reservation, California

Penobscot Tribe of Maine

Peoria Tribe of Oklahoma

Picayune Rancheria of Chukchansi Indians of California

Pinoleville Rancheria of Pomo Indians of California

Pit River Tribe of California
   Big Bend Rancheria
   Lookout Rancheria
   Montgomery Creek Rancheria
   Roaring Creek Rancheria
   XL Ranch

Poarch Creek Band of Creek Indians of Alabama

Pokagon Band of Potawatomi Indians of Michigan

Ponca Tribe of Indians of Oklahoma

Ponca Tribe of Nebraska

Port Gamble Community of the Port Gamble Reservation, Washington

Potter Valley Rancheria of Pomo Indians of California

Prairie Band of Potawatomi Indians of Kansas

Prairie Island Community of Minnesota Mdewakanton Sioux Indians of the Prairie Island Reservation, Minnesota

Pueblo of Acoma, New Mexico

Pueblo of Cochiti, New Mexico

Pueblo of Jemez, New Mexico

Pueblo of Isleta, New Mexico

Pueblo of Laguna, New Mexico

Pueblo of Nambe, New Mexico

Pueblo of Picuris, New Mexico

Pueblo of Pojoaque, New Mexico

Pueblo of San Felipe, New Mexico

Pueblo of San Ildefonso, New Mexico

Pueblo of San Juan, New Mexico

Pueblo of Sandia, New Mexico

Pueblo of Santa Ana, New Mexico

Pueblo of Santa Clara, New Mexico

Pueblo of Santo Domingo, New Mexico

Pueblo of Taos, New Mexico

Pueblo of Tesuque, New Mexico

Pueblo of Zia, New Mexico

Puyallup Tribe of the Puyallup Reservation, Washington

Pyramid Lake Paiute Tribe of the Pyramid Lake Reservation, Washington

Quapaw Tribe of Oklahoma

Quartz Valley Community of the Quartz Valley Reservation of California

Quechan Tribe of the Fort Yuma Reservation, California

Quileute Tribe of the Quileute Reservation, Washington

Quinault Tribe of the Quinault Reservation, Washington

Ramona Band or Village of Cahuilla Mission Indians of California

Red Cliff Band of Lake Superior Chippewa Indians of Wisconsin

Red Lake Band of Chippewa Indians of the Red Lake Reservation, Minnesota

Redding Rancheria of California

Redwood Valley Rancheria of Pomo Indians of California

Reno-Sparks Colony, Nevada

Rincon Band of Luiseno Mission Indians of the Rincon Reservation, California

Robinson Rancheria of Pomo Indians of California

Rosebud Sioux Tribe of the Rosebud Reservation, South Dakota

Round Valley Tribes of the Round Valley Reservation, California (formerly known as the Covelo Indian Community)

Rumsey Rancheria of Wintun Indians of California

Sac and Fox Tribe of the Mississippi in Iowa

Sac and Fox Nation of Missouri in Kansas and Nebraska

Sac and Fox Nation of Oklahoma

Saginaw Chippewa Tribe of Michigan, Isabella Reservation

St. Croix Chippewa Indians of Wisconsin, St. Croix Reservation

St. Regis Band of Mohawk Indians of New York

Salt River Pima-Maricopa Community of the Salt River Reservation, Arizona

San Carlos Apache Tribe of the San Carlos Reservation, Arizona

San Juan Southern Paiute Tribe of Arizona

San Manuel Band of Serrano Mission Indians of the San Manual Reservation, California

San Pasqual Band of Diegueno Mission Indians of California

Santa Rosa Community of the Santa Rosa Rancheria, California

Santa Rosa Band of Cahuilla Mission Indians of the Santa Rosa Reservation, California

Santa Ynez Band of Chumash Mission Indians of the Santa Ysabel Reservation, California

Santa Ysabel Band of Diegueno Mission Indians of the Santa Ysabel Reservation, California

Santee Sioux Tribe of the Santee Reservation of Nebraska

Sauk-Suiattle Tribe of Washington

Sault Ste. Marie Tribe of Chippewa Indians of Michigan

Scotts Valley Band of Pomo Indians of California

Seminole Nation of Oklahoma

Seminole Tribe of Florida, Dania, Big Cypress and Brighton Reservations

Seneca Nation of New York

Seneca-Cayuga Tribe of Oklahoma

Shakopee Mdewakanton Sioux Community of Minnesota (Prior Lake)

Sheep Ranch Rancheria of Me-Wuk (Miwok) Indians of California

Sherwood Valley Rancheria of Pomo Indians of California

Shingle Springs Band of Miwok Indians, Shingle Springs Rancheria (Verona Tract), California

Shoalwater Bay Tribe of the Shoalwater Bay Reservation, Washington

Shoshone Tribe of the Wind River Reservation, Wyoming

Shoshone-Bannock Tribes of the Fort Hall Reservation of Idaho

Shoshone-Paiute Tribes of the Duck Valley Reservation, Nevada

Sisseton-Wahpeton Sioux Tribe of the Lake Traverse Reservation, South Dakota

Skokomish Tribe of the Skokomish Reservation, Washington

Skull Valley Band of Goshute Indians of Utah

Smith River Rancheria of California

Soboba Band of Luiseno Mission Indians of the Soboba Reservation, California

Sokogoan Chippewa Community of the Mole Lake Band of Chippewa Indians, Wisconsin

Southern Ute Tribe of the Southern Ute Reservation, Colorado

Spokane Tribe of the Spokane Reservation, Washington

Squaxin Island Tribe of the Squaxin Island Reservation, Washington

Standing Rock Sioux Tribe of North and South Dakota

Stillaquamish Tribe of Washington

Stockbridge-Munsee Community of Mohican Indians of Wisconsin

Summit Lake Paiute Tribe of Nevada

Suquamish Tribe of the Port Madison Reservation, Washington

Susanville Rancheria of Paiute, Maidu, Pit River and Washoe Indians of California

Swinomish Indians of the Swinomish Reservation, Washington

Sycuan Band of Diegueno Mission Indians of California

Table Bluff Rancheria of Wiyot Indians of California

Table Mountain Rancheria of California

Te-Moak Tribes of Western Shoshone Indians of Nevada

Thlopthlocco Tribal Town of the Creek Nation of Oklahoma

Three Affiliated Tribes of the Fort Berthold Reservation, North Dakota

Tohono O'odham Nation of Arizona (formerly known as the Papago Tribe of the Sells, Gila Bend and San Xavier Reservation, Arizona)

Tonawanda Band of Seneca Indians of New York

Tonkawa Tribe of Indians of Oklahoma

Tonto Apache Tribe of Arizona

Torres-Martinez Band of Cahuilla Mission Indians of California

Tulalip Tribes of the Tulalip Reservation, Washington

Tule River Tribe of the Tule River Reservation, California

Tunica-Biloxi Tribe of Louisiana

Tuolumne Band of Me-Wuk (Miwok) Indians of the Tuolumne Rancheria of California

Turtle Mountain Band of Chippewa Indians of North Dakota

Tuscarora Nation of New York

Twentynine Palms Band of Luiseno Mission Indians of California

United Auburn Community of the Auburn Rancheria of California

United Keetoowah Band of Cherokee Indians of Oklahoma

Upper Lake Band of Pomo Indians of Upper Lake Rancheria of California

Upper Sioux Community of the Upper Sioux Reservation, Minnesota

Upper Skagit Tribe of Washington

Ute Tribe of the Uintah and Ouray Reservation, Utah

Ute Mountain Tribe of the Ute Mountain Reservation, Colorado, New Mexico and Utah

Utu Utu Gwaitu Paiute Tribe of the Benton Paiute Reservation, California

Viejas (Baron Long) Group of Capitan Grande Band of Mission Indians of the Viejas Reservation, California

Walker River Paiute Tribe of the Walker River Reservation, Nevada

Wampanoag Tribe of Gay Head (Aquinnah) of Massachusetts

Washoe Tribe of Nevada and California (Carson Colony, Dresslerville and Washoe Ranches)

White Mountain Apache Tribe of the Fort Apache Reservation, Arizona

Wichita and Affiliated Tribes (Wichita, Keechi, Waco and Tawakonie) of Oklahoma

Winnebago Tribe of Nebraska

Winnemucca Colony of Nevada

Wyandotte Tribe of Oklahoma

Yankton Sioux Tribe of South Dakota

Yavapai Apache Nation of the Camp Verde Reservation, Arizona

Yavapai-Prescott Tribe of the Yavapai Reservation, Arizona

Yerington Paiute Tribe of the Yerington Colony and Campbell Ranch, Nevada

Yomba Shoshone Tribe of the Yomba Reservation, Nevada

Ysleta Del Sur Pueblo of Texas

Yurok Tribe of the Yurok Reservation, California

Zuni Tribe of the Zuni Reservation, New Mexico

(*Note: The Chappaquiddick Wampanoag are not federally recognized*)

*Above:* This photograph of Seminole boatmen in the Florida Everglades near Miami was taken before 1921.

# APPENDIX IV.

# NATIVE NORTH AMERICAN ETHNICITY GROUPINGS

Ahtena of Alaska

Alabama-Coushatta (Alibamu, Koasati)
    Alabama-Coushatta Reservation of Texas
    Coushatta Tribe of Louisiana

Algonquin Nations
    Abenaki (Maine, Vermont, New York)
    Algonquin Bands of Quebec
    Mohican/Mahican (Stockbridge-Munsee)
    Odanak of Quebec
    Virginia Algonquin (Tidewater Area)

Apache (Athapaskan)
    Apache Tribe of Oklahoma (formerly known as
        Kiowa-Apache)
    Fort Sill Apache Tribe of Oklahoma
        (Chiricahua, Warm Springs)
    Jicarilla Apache Reservation of New Mexico
    Mescalero Apache Reservation of New Mexico
        (Chiricahua, Lipan, Mescalero)
    San Carlos Apache Reservation of Arizona
    Tonto Apache Indians of Arizona
    White Mountain Apache Tribe of Arizona
        (White Mountain, Cibecue)

Apache (Athapaskan/Yuman)
    Yavapai-Apache Community of the
        Camp Verde Reservation of Arizona
    Fort McDowell Mohave-Apache
        Reservation of Arizona

Arapaho
    Arapaho Nations of Oklahoma
    Wind River Reservation of Wyoming

Arikara

Assiniboine
    Bands of Alberta
    Fort Belknap Reservation of Montana
    Fort Peck Reservation of Montana

Bannock
    Fort Hall Reservation of Idaho

Beaver Dene Band of Alberta

Blackfeet
    Blackfeet Reservation of Montana
    Blood Band of Alberta
    Peigan Nation of Alberta
    Siksika Nation of Alberta

Blue Lake Rancheria of California

Caddo Nation of Oklahoma

Cahuilla Mission Indians (California)
    Agua Caliente Band of the Agua Caliente
        Reservation of Palm Springs
    Augustine Reservation
    Cabazon Band of the Cabazon Reservation
    Cahuilla Reservation
    Los Coyotes Reservation
    Morongo Reservation
    Ramona Band or Village
    Santa Rosa Rancheria
    Torres-Martinez Reservation

Carrier Nation of British Columbia

Catawba
    South Carolina
    Utah

Chehalis Reservation of Washington,
    Confederated Nations of

Cher-Ae Heights Community
    Trinidad Rancheria of California

Cherokee
    Cherokee Nation of Oklahoma
    Cherokee of Alabama
    Eastern Band of North Carolina
    Echota Cherokee of Alabama
    United Keetoowah Band of Oklahoma

Cheyenne
    Cheyenne of Oklahoma
    Northern Cheyenne Reservation of
        Montana

Chickahominy Nation
    Charles City County, Virginia
    Providence Forge, Virginia

Chickasaw Nation of Oklahoma

Chilcotin Nation of British Columbia

Chipewyan Dene Bands
    Alberta
    Manitoba
    Northwest Territories
    Saskatchewan

Chippewa (Ojibway)
    Bad River Reservation of Lake Superior,
Wisconsin
        Bay Mills Community of the Sault Ste. Marie
            of Bay Mills Reservation of Michigan
        Chippewa Indians of the Rocky Boy's
            Reservation of Montana
        Grand Traverse Band of Michigan
        Keweenaw Bay Community of L'Anse of
            Lac Vieux Desert and Ontonagon Bands
            of the L'Anse Reservation of Michigan
        Lac Courte Oreilles Band of Lake Superior of
            the Lac Courte Oreilles Reservation of
            Wisconsin
        Lac du Flambeau Band of Lake Superior of the
            Lac du Flambeau Reservation of
            Wisconsin
        Lac Vieux Desert Band of Michigan
        Minnesota Chippewa Nation of Minnesota
            Bois Forte Band of Nett Lake
            Fond du Lac Band
            Grand Portage Band
            Leech Lake Band
            Mille Lac Band
            White Earth Band
        Ojibway Bands and Reserves of Manitoba,
            Ontario, Quebec, Saskatchewan
        Red Cliff Band of Lake Superior of Red Cliff
            Reservation of Wisconsin
        Red Lake Band of the Red Lake Reservation of
            Minnesota
        Saginaw Nation of Michigan of Isabella
            Reservation of Michigan
        Sault Ste. Marie Nation of Michigan
        Sokogoan Community of the Mole Lake Band
            of Wisconsin
        St. Croix Reservation of Wisconsin
        Turtle Mountain Reservation of North Dakota

Chitimacha Nation of Louisiana

Choctaw
    Choctaw Nation of Oklahoma
    Mississippi Band of Choctaw Indians
    Mowa Band of Choctaws, Alabama

Chukchansi Indians of California, Picayune Rancheria

Chumash
    Santa Ynez Band of Mission Indians of California

Cocopah Nation of Arizona

Coeur D'Alene Reservation of Idaho

Colorado River Reservation of Arizona and
    California

Colville Reservation of Washington,
    Confederated Nations of

Comanche Nation of Oklahoma

Coos, Confederated Nations of
    Lower Umpqua
    Siuslaw

Covelo Community of the Round Valley
    Reservation of California

Cow Creek Band of Umpqua Indians of Oregon

Cree Nations
    Bands and Reserves of Alberta, Manitoba,
        Ontario, Quebec, Saskatchewan
    Plains Cree in northeastern Manitoba
    Rocky Boy's Reservation of Montana

Crow Nation of Montana

Dakota/Lakota/Nakota (Sioux)
    Canadian Bands of Manitoba and
        Saskatchewan
    Cheyenne River Reservation of South Dakota
    Crow Creek Reservation of South Dakota
    Devils Lake Sioux Reservation of North
        Dakota
    Flandreau Santee Sioux Nation of South Dakota
    Fort Peck Reservation of Montana
    Lower Brule Reservation of South Dakota
    Minnesota Mdewakanton Sioux Indians of the
        Lower Sioux Reservation in Minnesota
    Oglala Sioux Nation of the Pine Ridge
        Reservation of South Dakota
    Prairie Island Reservation of Minnesota
        (Mdewakanton Dakota)
    Rosebud Sioux Nation of the Rosebud
        Reservation of South Dakota
    Santee Sioux Nation of the Santee Reservation
        of Nebraska
    Shakopee Mdewakanton Sioux Community of
        Minnesota (Prior Lake)
    Sisseton-Wahpeton Sioux Nation of the Lake
        Traverse Reservation of South Dakota
    Standing Rock Sioux Nation of the Standing
        Rock Reservation of North and South
        Dakota
    Upper Sioux Community of the Upper
        Sioux Reservation of Minnesota
    Yankton Sioux Nation of South Dakota

Delaware Nation of Western Oklahoma

Dene-Dhaa Nation of British Columbia

Diegueno Mission Indians (California)
    Barona Capitan Grande Reservation
    Campo Reservation
    Capitan Grande Reservation
    Cuyapaipe Reservation
    Inaja and Cosmit Reservation

La Posta Reservation
Mesa Grande Reservation
San Pasqual Reservation
Santa Ysabel Reservation
Sycuan Reservation
Viejas Baron Long Capitan Grande Band of the
    Viejas Reservation

Dogrib Dene Bands of Northwest Territories

Dunne-Za Nation of British Columbia

Eastern Chickahominy (Virginia)

Eyak (Athapaskan) of Alaska

Fort Mohave Nation of Arizona

Gitksan Nation of British Columbia

Golden Hill Paugusset of Trumbull, Connecticut

Goshute Indians (Western Shoshone)
    Skull Valley Band of Utah
    Gila River Reservation of Arizona
    Goshute and Skull Valley Reservations of Utah
    Goshute Reservation of Nevada and Utah
        Confederated Nations of

Grand Ronde Community of Oregon,
    Confederated Nations of

Gros Ventre (Atsina)
    Fort Belknap Reservation of Montana

Gwich'in (Kutchin) Dene Bands of Alaska, Northwest
        Territories and Yukon

Haida
    Alaskan Communities
    Haida Nation of British Columbia

Haisla Nation of British Columbia

Haliwa-Saponi Nation, Hollister, North Carolina

Halkomelem Nation of British Columbia
    Burrard
    Homalko
    Saanich
    Squamish
    Stolo

Han (Athapaskan) of Alaska and Yukon Territory

Hare Dene Bands of the Northwest Territories

Havasupai Reservation of Arizona

Ho-Chunk (Winnebago)
    Reservation of Nebraska
    Reservation of Wisconsin

Hoh Reservation of Washington

Hoopa Valley Reservation of California

Hopi Nation of Arizona

Houma Indians of Louisiana

Hualapai Reservation of Arizona

Huron

Ingalik (Athapaskan) of Alaska

Inuit (formerly known as Eskimo)
    Alaska
    Labrador
    Northwest Territories
    Quebec

Iowa Nation of Oklahoma

Iowa Reservation in Nebraska and Kansas

Iroquois (Six Nations)
    Cayuga Nation of Versailles of New York
    Iroquois Band in Alberta
    Kanesatake (Mohawk) Band of Oka, Quebec
    Mohawks of Kahnawake of Quebec
    Oneida Nation of New York
    Oneida Nation of Wisconsin of
        Oneida Reservation of Wisconsin
    Onondaga Nation of Nedrow of New York
    Seneca Nation of Salamanca of New York
    Seneca-Cayuga Nation of Oklahoma
    St. Regis Band of Mohawk Indians of
        Hogansburg of New York
    Stockbridge-Munsee Community of Mohican
        Indians of Wisconsin
    Tonawanda Band of Seneca Indians of Basom
        of New York
    Tuscarora Nation of Lewiston of New York

Jamul Village of California

Karuk Nation of California

Kaska Dene
    Kaska Dene Nation of British Columbia
    Northwest Territories
    Yukon

Kato
    Laytonville Rancheria of California
    Trinidad Rancheria of California

Kaw Nation of Oklahoma

Kawaiisu (Tule Reservation, California)

Kickapoo
    Kickapoo Reservation in Kansas
    Oklahoma (includes Texas Band of Kickapoo
        Indians)

Klallam Indians of Washington
    Jamestown Band
    Lower Elwha S'Klallam Nation
    Port Gamble Nation (S'Klallam)

Klamath Indians
    Karok of Shasta, Quartz Valley Rancheria of
        California
    Klamath
    Modoc
    Yahooskin Band of Snake Indians

Kootenai (Kutenai)
    Flathead (Salish) Reservation in Montana
    Reservations in Idaho and Canada

Koyukon (Athapaskan) of Alaska

Ktunaxa-Kinbasket Nation (Kootenai) of British
    Columbia

Kwakiutl Nation of British Columbia

Lower Elwha Reservation of Washington

Luiseno Mission Indians (California)
    La Jolla Reservation
    Pala Reservation
    Pauma and Yuma Reservation
    Pechanga Reservation
    Rincon Reservation
    Soboba Reservation
    Twentynine Palms Reservation

Lumbee Nation, Robeson County, North Carolina

Lummi Reservation of Washington

Maidu Indians (California)
    Berry Creek Rancheria
    Enterprise Rancheria
    Greenville Rancheria
    Mooretown Rancheria
    Susanville Rancheria

Makah Reservation of Washington

Maliseet (Malecite) Indians
    Houlton Band (Maine)
    Bands in New Brunswick

Maricopa
    Ak Chin Community of Arizona
    Gila River Reservation of Arizona
    Salt River Reservation of Arizona

Mashantucket Pequot Nation of Ledyard of
    Connecticut

Mattaponi
    Mattaponi Reservation of West Point, Virginia
    Upper Mattaponi Nation, King William, Virginia

Mattole Indians of California
    Rohnerville Rancheria of Bear River

Menominee Reservation of Wisconsin

Miami Nation of Oklahoma

Miccosukee Nation of Indians of Florida

Micmac of New Brunswick and Nova Scotia

Miwok (California)
    Buena Vista Rancheria
    Chicken Ranch Rancheria
    Jackson Rancheria
    Sheep Ranch Rancheria
    Shingle Springs Band
    Tuolumne Rancheria

Miwok (California, Coast)
    Redwood Valley Rancheria
    Stewarts Point Rancheria

Modoc Nation of Oklahoma

Mohave
    Fort Mohave Tribe of Arizona

Mohican/Mohegan/ Mahican
    Mohegan Tribe of Uncasville, Connecticut
    Stockbridge-Munsee Reservation of Wisconsin

Mona Indians
    Big Sandy Rancheria

Monacan Nation, Amherst, Virginia

Mono Indians
    Cold Springs Rancheria

Muckleshoot Reservation of Washington

Muskogee (Creek) Nation
    Creek Nation of Oklahoma
    Alabama-Quassarte Tribal Town of Oklahoma
    Kialegee Tribal Town of Oklahoma
    Machis Lower Creek Tribe

Poarch Creek Band of Alabama
Star Clan of Muskogee Creek
Thlopthlocco Tribal Town of the Creek Nation
      of Oklahoma

Nansemond Nation, Driver, Virginia

Nanticoke Association of Millsboro, Delaware

Narragansett Nation of Charleston, Rhode Island

Navajo (Dinneh) of Arizona, New Mexico and Utah

Nez Perce Nation of Idaho

Nipmuck Nation of Hassanamico Reservation of
      Grafton, Massachusetts

Nisga'a Nation of British Columbia

Nlaka'pamux Nation (Thompson River) of British
      Columbia

Nisqually Community of the Nisqually
      Reservation of Washington

Nooksack Nation of Washington

Nuu-Chah-Nulth Nation (Nootka) of British
Columbia

Nuxalk Nation (Bella Coola) of British Columbia

Ojibway Nation (see Chippewa)

Okanagan Nation of British Columbia

Omaha Nation of Nebraska

Osage Nation of Oklahoma

Otoe-Missouri Nation of Oklahoma

Ottawa
      Grand Traverse Band of Michigan
      Little River Band of Michigan
      Little Traverse Bay Odawa Band of Michigan
      Ottawa Nation of Oklahoma

Paiute (Northern)
      Benton Paiute Reservation of California
      Big Pine Reservation of California

*Above:* A traditional Choctaw palmetto house on the shore of Lake Pontchartrain, circa 1881.

Bishop Community of the Bishop Colony of
    California
Bridgeport Colony of California
Burns Colony of Oregon
Carson Colony Community of Nevada
Cedarville Rancheria of California
Cold Springs Rancheria of California
Duck Valley Reservation of Nevada
Fallon Reservation and Colony of Nevada
Fort Bidwell Reservation of California
Fort Independence Reservation of California
Fort McDermitt Reservation of Nevada
Lone Pine Reservation of California
Lovelock Colony of Nevada
Mono Bridgeport Colony
Northfork Rancheria
Paiute Nation of Utah
Pit River Indians (except Southern Paiute)
Pyramid Lake Reservation of Nevada
Reno-Sparks Colony of Nevada
Stewart Colony of Nevada
Summit Lake Reservation of Nevada
Utu Utu Gwaitu of the Benton Paiute
    Reservation of California
Viejas Reservation of California
Walker River Reservation of Nevada
Winnemucca Colony of Nevada
Yerington Colony and Campbell Ranch

Paiute (Southern)
Chemehuevi of the Chemehuevi
Colorado River Reservations of Arizona
Kaibab Reservation of Arizona
Las Vegas Colony of Nevada
Moapa Reservation of Nevada
Paiute Tribe of Utah
San Juan Southern Paiute Tribe of Arizona

Pamunkey of Virginia

Papago (see also Tohono O'Odham)
Ak Chin Community of the Maricopa,
    Ak Chin Reservation, Arizona
Sells of Gila Bend and San Xavier Reservations
    of Arizona

Passamaquoddy
Indian Township Reservation of Princeton
Passamaquoddy Reservation of Perry, Maine

Paucatuck Pequot of Ledyard, Connecticut

Pawnee Nation of Oklahoma

Pelly Dene Bands of Yukon

Penobscot Nation of Old Town, Maine

Peoria Nation of Oklahoma

Pima
Gila River Reservation of Arizona
Salt River Reservation of Arizona

Pit River (Achomowi and Atsugewi)
Alturas Rancheria of California
Big Valley Rancheria of California
Dry Creek Rancheria of California
Las Vegas Nation of the Las Vegas
    Colony of Nevada
Lookout Rancheria of California
Manzanita Rancheria of California
Montgomery Creek Rancheria of California
Roaring Creek Rancheria of California
Susanville Rancheria of California
XL Ranch Reservation of California

Pomo
Big Valley Rancheria
Cloverdale Rancheria
Coyote Valley Band
Dry Creek Rancheria
Elem Colony
    of the Sulphur Bank Rancheria
Hopland Rancheria
Kashia Band
Manchester-Point Arena Rancheria
Middletown Rancheria
Pinoleville Rancheria
Potter Valley Rancheria
Redding Valley Rancheria
Robinson Rancheria
Sherwood Valley Rancheria
Upper Lake Rancheria

Ponca
Ponca Nation (Northern of Nebraska)
Ponca Tribe of Nebraska
Ponca Tribe of Oklahoma

Potawatomi Indians
Citizen Band of Oklahoma
Forest County Community of Wisconsin
Hannahville Community of Michigan
Pokagon Band of Michigan
Prairie Band of Holton, Kansas

Prairie Island Reservation of Minnesota

Pueblo
Acoma Pueblo
Cochiti Pueblo
Isleta Pueblo
Jemez Pueblo
Laguna Pueblo
Nambe Pueblo
Picuris Pueblo
Pojoaque Pueblo
San Felipe Pueblo

San Juan Pueblo
San Ildefonso Pueblo
Sandia Pueblo
Santa Ana Pueblo
Santa Clara Pueblo
Santo Domingo Pueblo
Taos Pueblo
Tesuque Pueblo
Ysleta Del Sur Pueblo
Zia Pueblo

Puyallup Reservation of Washington

Quapaw Nation of Oklahoma

Quechan Nation of the Fort Yuma Reservation
of California

Quileute Reservation of Washington

Quinault Reservation of Washington

Rappahannock Nation, King and Queen County,
Virginia

Reno-Sparks Colony of Nevada

Round Valley Tribes of Covelo, California

Sac and Fox Nation
Mississippi of the Sac and Fox Reservation of
Iowa
Missouri of the Sac and Fox Reservation of
Kansas and Nebraska
Sac and Fox Reservation of Oklahoma

Salish
Coeur D'Alene
Colville
Confederated Salish and Kootenai Nations of
the Flathead Reservation of Montana
Kalispel
Okanagan
Pend Orielle
Spokane Nation of the Spokane Reservation of
Washington

Salish (Coast) (see also Klallam)
Chehalis Reservation of Washington
Hoh Reservation of Washington
Klallam Reservation of Washington
Lower Elwha Reservation of Washington
Nooksack Reservation of Washington
Port Gamble Reservation of Washington
Puyallup Reservation of Washington
Quileute Reservation of Washington
Quinault Reservation of Washington
Sauk-Suiattle Reservation of Washington
Shoalwater Bay Reservation of Washington

Skokomish Reservation of Washington
Squaxin Island Reservation of Washington
Stillaquamish Reservation of Washington
Suquamish Reservation of Washington
Swinomish Reservation of Washington
Tulalip Reservation of Washington
Upper Skagit Reservation of Washington

Salt River Pima-Maricopa Reservation of Arizona

Santa Rosa Community of the Santa Rosa
Rancheria of California

Santa Ynez Band of Chumash Mission Indians of
California

Sarsi Reserve of Alberta

Sauk-Suiattle Nation of Washington

Schaghticoke Nation of Bristol, Connecticut

Secwepemc Nation (Shuswap) of British Columbia

Sekani
Sekani Dene
Sekani Nation of British Columbia

Seminole
Miccosukee Tribe of Florida
Seminole Nation of Oklahoma

Seminole Tribe of Florida, Dania, Big Cypress and
Brighton Reservations of Florida

Serrano Mission Indians of California (San Manuel
Band)

Shasta of the Quartz Valley Reservation of
California

Shawnee
Absentee of Oklahoma
Eastern Shawnee of Oklahoma

Shinnecock Reservation of Southampton, New York

Shoalwater Bay Reservation of Washington

Shoshone
Big Pine Reservation of California
Bishop Community of California
Death Valley Timbi-Sha of California
Duck Valley Reservation of Nevada
Duckwater Reservation of Nevada
Elko Band of Nevada
Ely Colony of Nevada
Fallon Reservation and Colony of Nevada
Fort McDermitt Reservation of Nevada

Lone Pine Reservation of California
Northwestern Band of Utah (Washakie)
Shoshone-Bannock Nations of the Fort Hall
    Reservation of Idaho
Shoshone-Paiute of Owyhee, Nevada
Te-Moak Bands of the Battle Mountain of Elko
    and South Fork Colonies of Nevada
Timba-sha Shoshone Tribe of Death Valley
Wells Colony of Nevada
Wind River Reservation of Wyoming
Yomba Reservation of Nevada

Siletz Reservation of Oregon, Confederated Nations of

Skokomish Reservation of Washington

Slave Dene Bands of Alberta and Northwest
    Territories

Smith River Tolowa Indians (California)
    Big Lagoon Rancheria
    Elk Valley Rancheria
    Smith River Rancheria

Squaxin Island Nation of the Squaxin Island
    Reservation of Washington

Stillaquamish Nation of Washington

Suquamish Nation of the Port Madison
    Reservation of Washington

Swinomish Reservation of Washington

Table Mountain Rancheria of California

Tahltan Dene
    Alaska and Yukon
    Tahltan Nation of British Columbia

Tanaina of Alaska

Tete de Boule Bands in Quebec

Three Affiliated Nations (North Dakota)
    Arikara
    Hidatsa
    Mandan

Tlingit
    Tagish
    Taku River

*Above:* The Zuni Pueblo as it appeared in 1879. The people of the Southwest built elaborate permanent cities.

Teslin
Tutchone

Tohono O'Odham (Papago)
    Gila River Reservation of Arizona
    Papago Reservation of Arizona

Tonkawa Nation of Indians of Oklahoma

Ts'ilhqot'in Nation (Chilcotin) of British Columbia

Tsimshian
    Alaskan communities
    Tsimshian Nation of British Columbia

Tulalip Reservation of Washington

Tule Reservation of California
    Kawaii
    Tubatulabal
    Vanyume

Tunica-Biloxi Nation of Louisiana

Tuscarora of North Carolina, Maxton, North Carolina

Umatilla Reservation of Oregon,
    Umatilla
    Walla Walla

Umpqua (see also Coos)

Ute
    Koosharem Reservation of Utah (Pavant)
    Southern Ute Reservation of Colorado
    Uintah and Ouray Reservation of Utah
    Ute Mountain Reservation of Colorado, New
        Mexico and Utah
    Ute (Southern) Nation of the Southern
    Ute Reservation of Colorado

Wampanoag Nation of Gay Head, Massachusetts

Warm Springs Reservation of Oregon,
    Confederated Nations of
            Wishram
            Weaco
            Puyallup-Pit River
            Cowlitz
            Klickitat
            Yakima-Klickitat
            Northern Paiute
            Upper Chinook

Washoe
    Dresslerville Community of Nevada
    Washoe Reservation of Nevada
    Winnemucca Colony of California
    Woodfords Community of California

Wet'suwet'en Nation of British Columbia

Wichita Nation of Oklahoma

Winnemucca Colony of Nevada

Wintun-Wailaki Indians (California)
    Cachil DeHe Band of the Colusa Rancheria
    Cortina Rancheria
    Grindstone Rancheria
    Rumsey Rancheria

Wiyot Indians of California
    Table Bluff Rancheria

Wyandotte Nation of Oklahoma
    Huron-Wendat Reserve (Eastern Quebec)

Yakima Nation of the Yakima Reservation of
    Washington, Confederated Bands of

Yaqui
    Yaqui-Pascua Nation of Arizona

Yavapai Prescott Reservation of Arizona
    Yavapai-Apache Tribe of Camp Verde
        Reservation, Arizona
    Mohave-Apache Tribe of Fort McDowell
        Reservation, Arizona

Yellowknives Dene Bands of Northwest Territories

Yokuts
    Big Sandy Rancheria of California

Yuchi Tribe of Oklahoma

Yurok (California)
    Blue Lake Rancheria of California
    Hoopa Valley Reservation
    Picayune Rancheria of California
    Resighini Rancheria
    Yurok Reservation of Eureka, California

Zia (see Pueblo)

Zuni Reservation of New Mexico

# INDEX

*Above:* Mountain Chief of the Blackfeet.